Whether it's a constant whisper or an ~~over-whelming~~ ~~shout,~~ we play in our head over and over can plague us for a lifetime. In *Quieting the Shout of Should*, Crystal Stine helps us identify the nagging lies we believe and replace them with the truth and freedom that is available to us in Christ today. If you find yourself trapped in the endless cycle of doubt, fear, comparison, and insecurity and are looking for a solid biblical approach to experiencing your life anew, this book is for you.

—**Ruth Schwenk**

Founder of TheBetterMom.com, cohost of *Rootlike Faith* podcast, coauthor of *In a Boat in the Middle of a Lake*

Crystal has done a clear job of identifying the *many* areas where women get defeated, carry guilt, or explain away how God has created them. She gives everyday examples that make me think she is reading my journal! Crystal provides practical, biblical ways to work through some of the lies and barriers we encounter. In a time when it's so easy to compare ourselves to others, it's a breath of fresh air to have someone give us permission to step into everything God has for each one of us uniquely!

—**Clare Smith**

Speaker, trainer, coach

It's hard enough trying to navigate life without constant reminders of how we're not doing it right. In her utterly upfront and expansive new book, *Quieting the Shout of Should*, Crystal reminds us our value to God is in who we are in His sight, not in who we or others think we should be. Crystal beautifully shares her own honest stories of faith and failure and how we can serve and love from a place of strength, not striving. Her wise words will provide readers practical actions and sound advice to quiet the shouts of should in our own lives.

—Kate Battistelli
Author of *The God Dare* and *Growing Great Kids*

The shout of should beats its angry drum louder than ever now. With clarity and grace, Crystal Stine leads us through the battlefields of life, uncovering expectations and realities that keep us from fully embracing what God has for us. This book is a crucial guide for anyone who desires to live past the boundaries of should in the land of freedom.

—Erin Moon
Author of *Every Broken Thing*, *The Comfortable Words*, and *O Heavy Lightness*

QUIETING

— THE SHOUT OF —

SHOULD

Crystal Stine

HARVEST HOUSE PUBLISHERS
EUGENE, OREGON

Cover by Faceout

Cover photo © Olya Fedorova / Shutterstock

Interior design by KUHN Design Group

Published in association with Books & Such Literary Management, 52 Mission Circle, Suite 122, PMB 170, Santa Rosa, CA 95409-5370, www.booksandsuch.com

For bulk, special sales, or ministry purchases, please call 1-800-547-8979 or email Customerservice@hhpbooks.com

Quieting the Shout of Should
Copyright © 2020 by Crystal Stine
Published by Harvest House Publishers
Eugene, Oregon 97408
www.harvesthousepublishers.com

ISBN 978-0-7369-8100-2 (pbk.)
ISBN 978-0-7369-8101-9 (eBook)

Library of Congress Cataloging-in-Publication Data

Names: Stine, Crystal, author.
Title: Quieting the shout of should / Crystal Stine.
Description: Eugene, Oregon : Harvest House Publishers, 2020. | Summary:
   "In this all-inclusive guide to letting go of the guilt and shame of
   trying to live up to what everyone else is doing, you will learn to
   quiet the shouts of should that keep you from moving toward God's plan
   for our life"-- Provided by publisher.
Identifiers: LCCN 2020012291 (print) | LCCN 2020012292 (ebook) | ISBN
   9780736981002 (pbk) | ISBN 9780736981019 (ebook)
Subjects: LCSH: Christian women--Religious life. | Guilt--Religious
   aspects--Christianity. | Guilt--Religious aspects--Christianity.
Classification: LCC BV4527 .S734955 2020 (print) | LCC BV4527 (ebook) |
   DDC 248.8/43--dc23
LC record available at https://lccn.loc.gov/2020012291
LC ebook record available at https://lccn.loc.gov/2020012292

Printed in the United States of America

20 21 22 23 24 25 26 27 28 / BP / 10 9 8 7 6 5 4 3 2 1

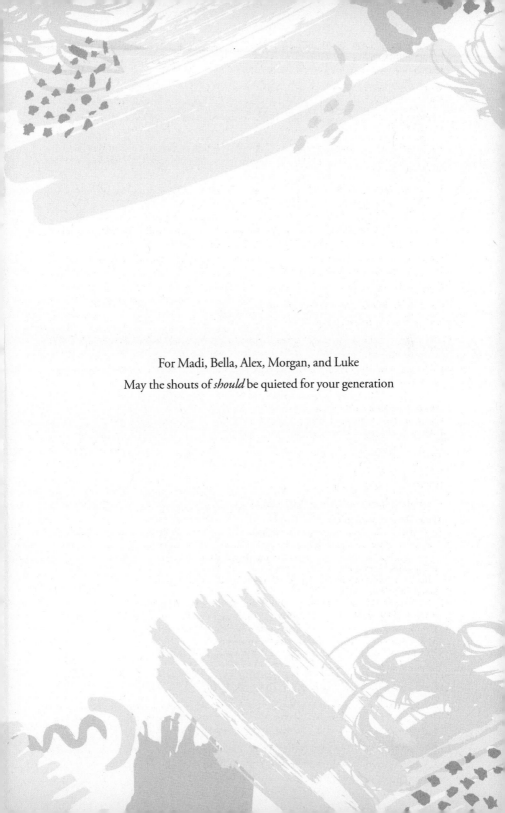

For Madi, Bella, Alex, Morgan, and Luke
May the shouts of *should* be quieted for your generation

Contents

Introduction

I have a constant soundtrack playing in my head. I wish I could tell you it was music (although "Carry On, Wayward Son" by Kansas is usually my earworm of choice), but unfortunately, my life is less spontaneous Disney musical and more to-do lists, doubts, expectations, demands, and dreams.

After speaking with women around the country, I know I'm not the only one who is looking for a way to quiet the shout of *should* from the world so we can fully embrace who God has created us to be. That's what this book is—not permission to put on headphones and check out from our lives, but an invitation to go on a journey that navigates the noise of the world as we swap what weighs us down for the quiet, uplifting guidance from God our souls seek. It's also not a simple self-help book where you'll finish the final chapter and have your life sorted out in a few easy steps. What you *will* discover is the ability to identify what, in your current season, is keeping you from living fully as a daughter of God.

There are a couple of ways you can read this book:

1. Read on your own.

Each chapter will introduce you to a specific should women struggle with and will include parts of my story, a deep dive into relevant scripture, and time at the end of each section for you to pause and connect with God.

2. Read with a group.

This book has also been designed with your book clubs and Bible studies in mind and includes reflection/discussion questions at the end of each chapter and a series of devotions to help you create a more personal experience. Is there work God is going to want you to do on your own, just with Him? Absolutely. Are we designed for community, and do we need to have women in our lives who can take these next steps with us? Definitely. You'll also find reading plans and additional book club materials at shoutofshouldbook.com.

At the end of each section you'll find an invitation to slow down and spend time in God's Word. In addition to the "Digging Deeper" sections in each chapter, these devotions will point you back to Scripture and invite you to create space to hear what God has to say to you. At the end of each devotion you'll find a challenge—a quest to find quiet in the midst of the chaos.

I hope you choose to read this book slowly, giving yourself time to rest and reflect and space to hear from God over all the shoulds the world shouts at you. Running on empty will never take you where God needs you, and listening to the shouts of should from the world will only distract you from living fully in God's peace, provision, and power. Refill and refuel so you can be prepared to do the work God has set before you with passion and joy. Let's get ready to silence some shoulds.

Part 1

Relationships

1

I Should Be More Like Her

Nobody wants to be *should* on.

Whether it's the world shouting a list of expectations and demands at us, social media showing us what life is like for someone else, or even a desire to fit in, twisting our dreams and goals, when we slow down long enough to really pay attention to the thoughts in our heads, we find we've been should on.

I've had countless opportunities over the years to experience the burden of should on my life. From college to married life, from the workplace to social media, I've found myself so thick in the expectations of others (and myself) that joy, peace, and contentment had no room to thrive.

It's easy for the best intentions of *should* to paralyze us from moving toward God's plan for our lives. We begin every year thinking that we should get healthy, or we should finally start that project we've always dreamed of doing. Before we know it, we find ourselves frustrated at our lack of progress and wondering why we haven't achieved what seemed simple for other women. What started as a good goal turns into a comparison trap that we struggle to escape.

As I've explored my struggles with should over the years, I've discovered that some deeper issues take me from living with an eternal perspective, holy anticipation, and healthy expectations to feeling like I've been should on: fear, insecurity, pride, comparison, doubt, and unrealistic expectations.

Fear tells me I should get moving because if I don't, I'll never achieve my dreams. Insecurity tells me I should change who I am and how I act because if I'm more like *her*, I'll feel confident, secure, and invited. Pride tells me I should do everything I can to keep up with the Joneses so I can be the best and shine the spotlight on myself—regardless of how hustling in that way burns out, wearies, and overwhelms me. Comparison tells me I should do more, be more—or else I've failed. Doubt tells me I should fake it until I make it because I'm not sure I belong or am good enough, but I can't let anyone else know it. And over it all is a layer of unrealistic expectations that my life, family, friends, work, and faith should look a certain way, and I should go to any length necessary to make every piece of my life practically perfect.

I'm exhausted just making that list.

That's what carrying the burden of should does to our lives. It keeps our eyes focused on everything—and everyone—around us instead of directing our gaze toward God. Should tries to yell so loudly in our ears that we can never hear God's voice inviting us to our next best step. Should is bossy and confusing and a liar. If should were a person, she would be someone your parents warned you to stay away from—the mean girl who makes you feel special for a little while but eventually turns on you.

Before we can break free from the chains of should, it would be helpful to understand why it's so hard to change how we think—about our lives, our circumstances, and ourselves. There is a good reason it's difficult to break up with should.

Blame it on your brain.

Scripture tells us that our words are an overflow of our hearts (Luke 6:45). How we speak—to others and ourselves—is a reflection of what is in our hearts. Our thoughts follow our hearts, and our words follow our thoughts.

Maybe you've heard it like this: "garbage in, garbage out." Hearts that are focused on the expectations and demands of the world will bear bad fruit. But hearts filled with God, grace, and the gospel bear good fruit in thought, word, and action. Through salvation and with God's help, we can be—as the apostle Paul says in Romans 12:2— transformed by the renewing of our minds.

And that transformation can make the difference between surviving and thriving. It's been said that Satan doesn't need to destroy us, only distract us, to keep us from fulfilling the plans God has for us. What better way than to distract us with the noise of the world, filling our hearts and minds with all the things we think we should be doing, ensuring we miss out on the fulfilling work God has for us?

Science tells us that our thoughts create patterns that change the landscape of our brains, cells, and genes. One writer explains the way our brain changes based on our thoughts:

> What flows through your mind also sculpts your brain in permanent ways. Think of your mind as the movement of information through your nervous system… As a thought travels through your brain, neurons fire together in distinctive ways based on the specific information being handled,

and those patterns of neural activity actually change your neural structure.

Busy regions of the brain start making new connections with each other, and existing synapses, the connections between neurons, that experience more activity get stronger, increasingly sensitive, and start building more receptors. New synapses are also formed.[1]

Whether looking to Scripture or science, do you want to know the best part? With God, we can change the direction of our thoughts, create new patterns in our brains, and quiet the shout of should in our lives. It's possible, but we can't do it on our own. All the idols that should has built up in our lives need to be torn down to make room for abiding with Jesus, serving His kingdom with confidence and peace.

I sat on the carpeted floor of a small room in a building that was part college dorm, part nursing college. It was freshman orientation, and I felt a combination of excitement, nervousness, and confidence. My dreams were coming true, and I was so proud of what I had already accomplished. A small-town girl making it into a prestigious university.

I had no idea what I was getting myself into.

Several upperclassmen were seated at the front of the room, sharing their stories. They encouraged us to join campus organizations and let us know that it was okay to be nervous about starting something new. And then a girl talked about coming from a small town and struggling to fit in because she couldn't afford the name-brand, high-end clothing that everyone around her was wearing. She shared her journey of discovering that her identity had nothing to do with the clothes she wore or all the things she thought she should do to fit in and make friends. Shopping at Kmart instead of Burberry no longer made her feel less-than because she'd learned that true friends wouldn't care what she wore or how much money she had.

I didn't get it, not really. I'd never been around that kind of privilege or prestige before, so why wouldn't someone feel comfortable wearing clothes from Kmart or Old Navy?

Moving into my dorm room in that same building quickly showed me how little I knew. The decorations I'd chosen for my room were looked down upon by my roommate and her mom. The clothes I thought were so great could never measure up to the preppy, labeled look of the girls in my hall. Without the experiences of spring break in Aspen, years of horseback riding lessons, and having a family with a beach house (or two), I struggled to find common ground.

I'd only been a Christian for a few years and didn't know what it meant to find my confidence in God. I wondered if going into debt purchasing clothes would help me feel like I belonged. Or maybe making the "right" friends who would include me in their vacations at beach houses and retreats in the mountains would make me feel less alone, or less...less-than.

When it came time for new leaders to be chosen for those retreats—the ones where we went to connect, unplug, and spend time with God—I applied. It was what I thought I should do. My expectations were high because I'd become friends with all the other leaders and those who planned the retreat. Of course I would be chosen! So I signed up to lead—over and over again. Each time an email was sent with the list of leaders and I wasn't on it, I became more discouraged.

My insecurity and fears made me desperate. I felt I should be chosen. I had experience and all the right friends, and I did all the right "faith things." But they never chose me.

In my power, nothing I could ever do would make me more like *her*—someone who would be picked. I could go into as much debt as I wanted, wear all the right clothes, have all the right friends, and behave in the way I thought I should to fit in…and none of it would ever be enough.

In those months of focusing on trying to be good enough for one group, I missed out on trying new things and building relationships with other women.

Trying to be who the world tells us we should be will only tear us down. What friendships do we miss because we're so caught up in the ones we think we should have? What experiences do we miss because we're so focused on being chosen for just one position?

Don't get me wrong, those five years I spent at college were full of amazing memories. But all my work trying to be someone else left me feeling left out, lonely, and depressed. I wasn't a good friend because I didn't know what kind of friend I was meant to be. I didn't thrive or try all the activities that interested me because I thought I should be doing something else.

I'd always been interested in sororities and the strong bonds those women had with one another, but I never joined one out of fear. I did, however, join the campus gospel choir, even though I can't actually sing, because other friends were joining and I didn't want to feel excluded. I chose not to study abroad in Ireland, something I'd always dreamed about, because I didn't want to disrupt my comfortable relationships or roommate plans. I did, however, start my freshman year in an international business relations course, because "business" seemed like a degree that would land me a great job after graduation—and I spent the next several months dreading the class, the professor, and the first truly bad grade I'd ever receive.

Trying to be like *her* only made me less of the woman God intended for me to be.

When we quiet the shout of should that tells us we need to be like someone else, we can embrace the identity God has given us with joy and peace.

Trying to be like *her* only made me less of
the woman God intended for me to be.

Digging Deeper

> One who heard us was a woman named Lydia, from the city of Thyatira, a seller of purple goods, who was a worshiper of God. The Lord opened her heart to pay attention to what was said by Paul. And after she was baptized, and her household as well, she urged us, saying, "If you have judged me to be faithful to the Lord, come to my house and stay." And she prevailed upon us.
>
> ACTS 16:14-15 ESV

In Acts 16 we read about Paul, Timothy, Silas, and Luke visiting Philippi. Paul's ministry had finally reached Europe, and this was their first stop to preach.[2] With no formal synagogue in the town (something that required ten Jewish men to start), the men found themselves at the riverside. They began to share with the women who had gathered there to pray, read from the Old Testament, and talk about what they had learned. John MacArthur notes, "It is significant that the first people Paul preached to in Europe were women."[3] Among them was Lydia, one of the first converts to Christianity.

Matthew Henry's commentary[4] notes four significant points about this passage:

1. *She was named.* Women aren't often named in the Bible, and when they are, it's significant.

2. *Her calling was identified.* Lydia's work is named and celebrated. The purple cloth that she sold would have been used by important figures in the Roman Empire—the wealthy and the royal. Though she was not wearing the garments herself, her work was honest and something to be proud of.

3. *She took advantage of where God placed her.* Although far from where she was born, her location was subservient to God's providence. When the opportunity for salvation and life-change presented itself, Lydia leaned in and took advantage of the invitation.

4. *Her faith opened her heart.* Luke's description of Lydia's response in verse 14 beautifully captures the way we respond to God's invitation. It's not one-sided, but rather a willingness to listen when God opens our heart—and then act on what our faith has shown us.

Lydia didn't simply sit by the waterside and listen to a nice story told by some travelers. She came to the Sabbath with a seeking heart and was ready to listen and act on what God was doing in her heart.

After hearing and believing, Lydia was baptized along with her household. They made a public profession of their faith, which Lydia followed with an invitation for the men to come and stay at her home. In the words of John MacArthur, "To make a home where travelers could be exposed to Christian love, family life, and fellowship was a high priority for Christian women (see 1 Timothy 5:9-10). Lydia's hospitality gave proof that she was a truly liberated woman."[5] It was obedience, openness, and availability that changed the course of her household forever—not acting a certain way or trying to be perfect.

What if Lydia had held back? What if she had looked around her at the other women along the river and decided she would only respond if they did? That group mentality comes with a choice: conform and stay comfortable or be courageous and stand out, even if it means standing alone. Going along with what everyone else is doing is another should that keeps us from living in the freedom and joy God has for us. Lydia knew God and studied His Word, and she was not so distracted by what everyone else was doing or thinking that she missed an opportunity to say "yes" to God.

As Lydia invited Paul, Timothy, Silas, and Luke into her home, she was not only offering hospitality to the travelers, but giving herself and her household the opportunity to ask questions, listen, and learn. As Matthew Henry puts it, "Those that know something of Christ cannot but desire to know more."[6] Lydia loved God so much that she accepted Jesus as her Savior and opened her home and heart to learn as much as she could from the apostles. She didn't have an example to look to for these actions, but she was confident enough in who she was as God's daughter to say "yes" even when no one else was making a move.

Has God brought you to a place you've been praying for, and now you feel stuck, trapped by comparison? What if He has you at the riverside to be refreshed in the presence of fellow believers? Could your time among women with similar passions, beliefs, and talents be an opportunity to learn, grow, and listen? Instead of being so distracted by what everyone else is doing, the opportunities they're sharing, and the ways you think you should be more like *her*, what if you entered into this particular season with a heart open to God's Word? What if you had ears ready to hear in holy anticipation what God has for you and a willingness to jump in with both feet when He extends the invitation?

> **What if you had ears ready to hear in holy anticipation what God has for you and a willingness to jump in with both feet when He extends the invitation?**

Quieting the shout of should in your life isn't just beneficial for you. Imagine the impact it might have on your family and your future if you were able to walk in the freedom of making choices that honor God, instead of trying to live up to what everyone else is doing. There is freedom and abundant living in choosing to embrace who God made you to be.

We aren't enough on our own, and we'll certainly never be perfect. But with God working in us and through us, we can be women who keep our eyes only on Christ, listening to who He says we are and putting our faith into action in ways that honor God—and who He made us to be.

Does this should show up for you at work? At church? When you're trying to figure out how to express the unique way God created you to worship or serve or lead? This should manifests itself every time you make a small change to fit in, hide just a little more of yourself, go along with what others are doing in hopes of an invitation to the table. It looks like choosing a group of *hers* over the call of God.

How do you fight it? One small choice at a time. One unapologetic yes to God when He calls your heart toward something new and unknown. One encouraging word to a woman who chooses to stand out instead of fitting in. One moment to affirm the unique, beautiful gift you see in someone else.

You, my friend, have been created by God. Not to fit in, but to be set apart. Choose every day to let your light shine and surround yourself with wise, trusted people who affirm who God made you to be. We can be women who quiet this should as we create groups and build friendships that welcome one another—just as God made us.

Flip the Script

Now that we've spent time together discussing this first should and digging into a biblical example, I want you to walk away feeling equipped to quiet the shout of should in your life. Below you'll find three real-life examples of how the should from this chapter might show up in your life, along with a "flip" suggestion—so you can turn over the should to God and refocus your heart.

- Flip "You should change how you look to fit in" to "God, thank You for designing me to be set apart so others see You."

- Flip "You should join that group if you ever want to be a leader" to "God, help me lead well right where I am."

- Flip "You should chase down that opportunity if you want to get ahead" to "God, I trust You to open the right doors at the right time."

Reflection / Book Club

I'm not going to pretend that any of this is easy. Retraining our brains? Identifying and silencing the noise that distracts us from joy? I wish I could tell you that this is a simple ten-step book that will give you all the tools you need to live a perfect, balanced, doubt-free life.

It's not.

"But with God all things are possible" (Matthew 19:26 ESV). You can read as many books as you'd like, get advice from friends, pay for courses, and join all the groups, but unless you're willing to learn, listen, and obey like Lydia, the noise of the world will only become louder and more oppressive. There is no one-size-fits-all solution because God didn't create us to be one-size-fits-all women.

1. When you consider all the noise around you, what is keeping you from hearing God?

2. How might your relationships—with God, friends, family, and your community—be different if you all committed to dropping the lies of should?

3. Describe a time when believing you should be more like *her* held you back from an opportunity God had for you.

> *Lord, thank You for so carefully and beautifully creating each of us in Your image. You are infinitely more creative than we could ever imagine. We can't do any of this without You. Guide our hearts as we retrain our minds. Create in us a holy anticipation of what You're about to do in us and through us as we seek You and open our hearts to all You have for us. In Jesus' name, amen.*

2

I Should Be a Better Mother

My daughter lost her arm at the dentist's.

There aren't many areas in motherhood where I've felt the impact of the "mommy wars"—not because I've figured out the secret to raising a perfectly well-behaved child, but because I'm pretty sure this is the least accomplished I've ever been at something. It's hard to feel like you need to defend your position on mothering when you're perfectly willing and excited to listen to *all* the ideas, podcasts, books, and other moms who have come before you and are offering advice.

But if there would be one tiny, itty-bitty area of being a mom that I was going to be proud of, it would be my daughter's teeth. Weird, right? My own experience with dentists has been long and complex. A simple scheduled cleaning visit where I don't need to book a return appointment is cause for celebration, so I didn't want my daughter to grow up with the same experience. We would brush her teeth diligently! She would have a cute light-up electric toothbrush that buzzes so she knows *exactly* how long to brush her teeth! I would download an app that plays music and games while she brushes to keep her entertained (two minutes is a long time, you guys)!

On her second visit to the dentist to have a cavity filled (after she'd already had a baby root canal and a follow-up appointment for a second cavity), she lost her arm. That was the subject of the text I received from my husband, who was nearly ready to upload a video of her—in all her laughing-gas glory—on the Internet so she could go viral.

Laughing gas may help some children relax, but ours gets a little antsy. This time she had taken her favorite "Bear Bear" with her but lost him under the paper bib she was wearing. In her search to find him, she believed she lost her arm.

She found it a few minutes later, still attached—don't worry.

Caring for another human being—whether a child, an ailing spouse, or an aging parent—can send us into a panic. We start looking everywhere and to everything we think might give us an answer, an assurance, or some hope. When our plans that we so carefully created aren't working out the way we thought they would, we scramble, forgetting that we have a Father who is right there with us—not laughing or capturing our moments on video, but drawing us near so that we can quiet the shouts of should and be the women He created us to be.

The struggle to overcome the shoulds of motherhood is one all women face, because we all nurture, care for, raise, mentor, lead, or invest in other human beings in some capacity. You might have a biological child, an adopted child, a foster child you've opened your home to, a niece or nephew, kids in your community, a church youth group, or a younger woman at your workplace you've chosen to mentor. Motherhood has one name but endless definitions.

Because motherhood brings with it the need to love and protect another human to the best of our ability, we can find ourselves a bit defensive when we receive unsolicited advice, raised eyebrows, and alarmingly personal questions from strangers. But motherhood can also open the door to an endless stream of shoulds as we look at our friends, other moms in our communities, and even celebrities and compare our parenting choices.

Studies have been done over the decades to try to determine the root of comparison. *Is it new? Is it because of social media? Should I throw away all my technology and become a hermit?* The answer to all of that is no. Comparison is a tool that has been used since the earliest days of humanity to evaluate and identify who we are, how we can serve, and what we're good at. And we get to choose whether or not we use it in a positive or negative way.

Imagine comparison as a superhero power. Like any good action star, you've come to a place where you must decide how you're going to use your gift. Will you use it for good, working hard to embrace a kind of "upward" comparison that will help you grow, improve, connect, and dream? Or will you use your comparison gift and serve the dark side—putting yourself higher than others, focusing on what you lack, and drifting away from community?

We tend to feel more emotionally tied to comparison when we're looking at someone else in a similar stage or season of life. Viewing what a recent college graduate is doing on Instagram certainly doesn't make me think I should be a better mother. But following another mom who promises that her style of parenting is the only way to raise a truly successful child makes me doubt the choices my husband and I have made as parents. Suddenly I find myself thinking...

- *I should choose that style of education.*

- *I should be a fun mom.*

- *I should enroll my daughter in all the classes to help her figure out what she loves.*

- *I should buy her more things.*

- *I should buy her fewer things.*

- *I should encourage her more.*

- *I should discipline her more.*

The list goes on and on, even for someone who has never been overly invested in "mommy wars." Social media and the ability to see into the lives of more people than ever before shape how we view ourselves. We now have a brand-new arena of comparison to enter, one where we're not simply connected to those in our real-life circles, but also millions of people online from all seasons, stages, and places.

The choice to focus on "upward" comparison becomes even more challenging when we're faced with topics we never even knew we should consider, like kids' birthday party decorations or the family vacations of people we haven't spoken to in a decade. The more we expose ourselves to the wide world of Internet wonder, without boundaries and a secure sense of who God made us to be, the more we will find ourselves spiraling. Suddenly our identity is wrapped up in our inability to decorate cookies and, in the noise, we lose the ability to focus and grow. It's our kryptonite.

Consider something as innocent as a gender reveal party. This phenomenon, which didn't exist in our collective vocabulary until a few years ago, quickly turned from a fun way to eat colorful cake to an outrageous display that, in one example, started a 47,000-acre wildfire.[1]

There is peace to be found in simplicity.

If there is good news to come out of all this, it's that we compare ourselves less as we get older because, as writer Rebecca Webber puts it when discussing the findings of a 2015 study, "We're more likely to evaluate ourselves against the yardstick of our own past rather than the present state of others."[2] Praise God! There is hope.

I promise you won't find a list of all the ways you should be a mother in this chapter. I'm still trying to figure it out, so as we navigate these pages and the shoulds that scream at us from the sidelines, we can give one another the grace and room to lean into where God is leading, whatever motherhood looks like for each of us. If we're going to compare, let's compare "up" to be inspired and motivated by God's example of selfless, tireless, endless love.

"You must be so excited to be done with work!" She was sweet and elderly and meant well as we stood talking between the pews after the church service was over on Sunday. It was a hard statement for me to address, not only because I wasn't sure that I really was excited, but also because she had already decided for me that I should be. I was nearing my due date and did, in fact, have several weeks of maternity leave coming up—but what this woman really meant was, "You must be so excited to be a stay-at-home mom!" How do I know that? Because when I shared with her that I was looking forward to getting back to the job I loved after my leave was over, she looked shocked and offended. My version of motherhood was not lining up with her expectations for me, and I hadn't even given birth to our daughter yet!

Staying at home with my daughter was the first of many shoulds I've experienced in parenting. The reality was, I knew how to do a great job at work—and I had no idea what I was doing when it came to being a mom. Over the years I've read the books, talked to friends, watched other women who look like they have it all figured out, attended conferences, and I still feel like a beginner.

I was already going into motherhood feeling like a failure after our first pregnancy ended in a miscarriage. I had finally started to believe that my body could do what it was meant to do while our daughter was on the inside, but I was 99 percent sure I had no idea what to do when she was actually here.

There's no handbook for investing in the life of a child. There are guidelines that tell me how many hours of sleep my child should get each night and statistics that remind me how important it is to read with her every day, but there are no rules about how much fun I need to be or what it really means to be a "good mom." How many times am I allowed to mess up before it's too many?

Searching for the answer to that question often finds me looking around at what the women around me are doing. I see the list of activities her children are in and wonder if I should sign up my daughter for more. I hear about the birthday party another mom held and wonder if I should do more for my family next year. I observe how her children are outgoing and friendly and wonder if I should encourage my shy, introverted child to be more like them—or maybe we should have more children? I see commercials where moms find a way to spend an entire afternoon playing make-believe and dressing up and I wonder if I should be more fun.

The world pushes us to question every idea and doubt every decision. It's not wrong to want to be a better mother, but when we try to be better than everyone else, we're failing ourselves and our kids.

When we don't know who we are in Christ we can allow the shoulds to distract us from our purpose. All I need to do is look outside at our garden to be reminded that God is wonderfully creative. Yes, each plant in our garden is technically a flower, but they each express their true form in a unique way. Different heights, colors, scents. Some need more sun than others, and some only bloom for a few short days, while others flower for an entire season. When we embrace the unique way God designed each of us to mother—and whom He calls us to nurture—we can break the cycle of should and watch the next generation bloom beautifully.

It takes courage to quiet the shout of should that tells us we're doing all the wrong things with the people God has placed in our lives. It takes courage to trust that He has given them to us for a reason. God has chosen you to love and lead those little people, and you can have faith that His expectations for you are reasonable and reachable and full of grace.

It's not wrong to want to be a better mother, but when we try to be better than everyone else, we're failing ourselves and our kids.

Digging Deeper

> I am a woman with a broken heart. I haven't had any
> wine or beer; I've been pouring out my heart before the

Lord. Don't think of me as a wicked woman; I've been
praying from the depth of my anguish and resentment.

1 Samuel 1:15-16

Have you ever wanted something so badly that you would promise almost anything to get it? Maybe it's a job you've been dreaming about since you were little or the perfect opportunity that will take your business to the next level. If you have children, you might have heard begging requests for a pet with promises about how responsible they'll be if you just say "yes." Or maybe, like the woman in today's passage, you've spent countless hours, days, and years in prayer asking God to give you the child your heart has been longing for.

"God, if you would just _____, I promise I will
_____."

Have you ever prayed something that like? I have. I could fill in those blanks with jobs I've wanted, family situations I've needed God's help with, issues with friends, and desires of my heart that exhausted all my own efforts.

In the book of 1 Samuel we read about a woman named Hannah who turned to God, made a sincere promise, and kept it when God answered her prayer.

Hannah shows us how we can transform our doubts and disappointments by handing over our dreams and desires to God. In a world that shouted shoulds at her because she couldn't live up to the expectations of the society she lived in—she should have had children by that point, she should have been fine with her husband's other wife, she should have prayed like everyone else—she was mocked, scorned, and desperate. But with sincere worship, prayer, and faith in God, Hannah found peace and—eventually—an answer to her prayers (1 Samuel 1:19-20).

What have you stopped asking God for? What area of your life are you still trying to control, to make things happen in your own timing and strength? What scary, life-changing dream has God given you that you need Him to say "yes" to so you can bring something amazing into the world?

Have you prayed about it?

Hannah's story is a beautiful reminder that God knows exactly the kind of heartache we'll experience in our lives. Some of us might relate to Hannah's story specifically as we wait to become mothers. Some of us might see ourselves more in her desperate prayers and promises—or maybe we've also felt left out, mocked, and unable to live up to the shoulds of the culture around us. Hannah gives us an example of choosing to make our lives less about us and more about God. As one devotional writer puts it, "Hannah's habit of prayer was less about her goodness and more about God's greatness."[3]

And Hannah's prayer didn't fall on deaf ears. Eli, the high priest, heard her prayer and gave her a gentle word of encouragement: "Go in peace, and may the God of Israel grant you what you have asked of him" (1 Samuel 1:17 NIV).

It takes a village. When our doubts are multiplied by the opinions, insensitive comments, and pressure of those around us, we can find ourselves retreating and alone. But even just one word of encouragement for our circumstances, as Eli gave to Hannah, can be just the thing we need to rejoin our communities with our heads held high. It takes a village—not just to raise a child, but to nurture God-given dreams.

No matter where we are in our motherhood journey, Hannah

reminds us that prayer should always be our first resort. It is that connection and obedience to God that will silence the shout of should. This should—to be a better mother—pulls on our maternal instinct to protect our children and tells us that there is only one right way. The should shouted at Hannah told her to keep her son close. She'd waited so long for him; she should raise him and do everything in her power to protect him. But Hannah walked closely with God and knew that the safest place her son could be was in God's hands.

When we have our prayers answered, what do we do? Do we move on to the next thing we want, or—like Hannah—do we give that blessing right back to the Lord (see 1 Samuel 1:21-28)? How hard it must have been to keep that promise to dedicate her son to the Lord and send him away! And yet she praised God and prayed, putting all the glory and focus back on Him:

> My heart rejoices in the LORD…
> There is no one holy like the LORD.
> There is no one besides you!
> And there is no rock like our God (1 Samuel 2:1-2).

Hannah's story is one of a woman who went before God with the desire of her heart, kept her promise when He said "yes," and turned all the glory and honor back on Him, where it belonged. And her son? The one she named Samuel because his name meant "asked of God"? He went on to lead the people of Israel, anointing Israel's first two kings, Saul and David.

This gift we've been given, to help children reach the fullness of who God created them to be, has eternal significance. Motherhood is a complex and unending series of choices, and our decisions not only keep our children clothed, fed, and loved, but also point them toward Jesus. And there is nothing that compares to what God can do through the life of one of His children. When the world shouts that we should be better mothers, or mother differently, or mother at all, we can go before God in prayer, knowing that He is faithful, He knows our story, and there is no one like Him.

> **May the shouts of the world be drowned out by our praise for You.**

Flip the Script

- Flip "You should only consider yourself a mother if you have children" to "God, thank You for giving me the opportunity to nurture and love the little ones in my life well."

- Flip "You should only feed/educate/clothe your child in one way" to "God, You are endlessly creative, never expecting us to be 'one size fits all,' and I'm so grateful that You have given us so many unique ways to raise a child."

- Flip "You should want to stay at home with your family" to "God, help me lean into the gifts You've given me so I can serve you and honor my family with freedom and joy."

Reflection / Book Club

As we seek God's wisdom to create a noiseless, joyful life that hears God above all else, there will be some areas that feel more challenging to hand over to Him. If you've been a Christian for more than five minutes, you've probably experienced seasons where you've felt like Hannah—in desperate prayer for the dreams on your heart, wondering when or if God will answer. Know that you aren't alone. God has given us examples and stories all throughout the Bible to remind us that we can discover more peace and less noise when we spend more time with Him, trusting Him with the details, dreams, and desires of our lives.

1. How would you fill in the blanks of this prayer? "God, if you would just _____, I promise I will _____."

2. How does having an eternal perspective on mothering—the impact and legacy your leadership and love could have on the next generation—help you silence should?

3. Talk about the last time you felt the pressure of the world weighing down on your parenting choices. Did you change what you were doing to fit in? How do you determine if you're receiving healthy, helpful advice or critical, judgmental feedback?

4. Brainstorm a few ways women can come together as a village to help one another's dreams thrive in this noisy world.

Father, thank You for knowing the dreams and desires of our hearts even before we've ever thought of them. Help us come to You first with our prayers, trusting that You will hear us, You are for us, and You will answer us— in Your perfect timing and way. May the shouts of the world be drowned out by our praise for You, and may we become women who lift one another up and keep each other connected in community. In Jesus' name, amen.

3

I Should Have More Friends

When I was in junior high school, I had an ongoing feud with a girl we'll call Kate. This was before social media gave kids the chance to bully one another through the protection of a computer screen, back when messaging a friend meant learning to write a note and fold it into a small square, corners all tucked in, so we could pass it quickly and privately between classes.

So we went after one another the old-fashioned way. We had a "burn book."

Ugh. I *know*. And this was before the movie *Mean Girls* came out, so I'm not sure how in the world we discovered that this was even a thing. But there it was, a book in which to write all our worst thoughts about people. I think those thoughts were supposed to be kept a secret, but in our small-town school the book was more like a shared journal. Back and forth we would go, writing down just the absolute worst things about one another. She would insult my intelligence and I would insult her style. We went after the attributes that felt the most precious to a teenage girl trying to sort out her identity, and it was a no-holds-barred mutual attack.

Kate was incredibly creative, comfortable in her own skin, an artist who dressed differently and seemed not to care what anyone else thought. I was a band geek who loved reading, tried to dress in current trends, and cared far too much about what other people thought. In junior high it felt like our feud lasted a lifetime. In reality? I think it fizzled out after a few months. It's a lot of work to fight with someone that long, and our mutual friends were becoming frustrated and annoyed with us.

Kate and I actually had a lot in common beyond our love of burning each other in that book. We shared a similar sense of humor, an appreciation for the arts, and a love of creativity. When we finally stopped focusing on what made us different, we started to appreciate what we had in common. By the time we finished high school, we had become the most unlikely friends.

I assumed (incorrectly) that it would be much easier to make and keep friends once I was an adult.

Friendship is a lot like a book. We know we shouldn't judge a book—or a new friend—by the cover, but we all do it. Our past experiences, expectations, and assumptions come along for the ride. And on top of that pile of baggage are the shoulds that shout at us from books, movies and television shows, and social media. Instead of feeling confident and comfortable in our ability to invest in a few deep friendships, we find our inner monologue shouting things like…

- *I should be good at making friends by now.*

- *I should have more friends.*

- *I shouldn't lose friends so easily.*

- *I should feel more included.*

- *I shouldn't have to plan get-togethers all the time.*

- *I should spend more time with my friends.*

- *Everyone else is better at making friends than me.*

Maybe you've had a few of those shoulds running through your head too. In this chapter we're going to explore how a life of fewer expectations can really lead to more as we take a look at the model of friendship God gives us in Scripture. We'll also burn a few of those shoulds along the way.

Psychologist Suzanne Degges-White defined friendship this way: "True friendships are hallmarked by each member's desire to engage with the other—it's about mutual interest in one another's experiences and thoughts, as well as a sense of 'belongingness' and connection. Friendships require reciprocity—of admiration, respect, trust, and emotional and instrumental support."[1]

I can watch my daughter make friends at the pool based on a desire to engage with someone; she needs a friend to play with and that girl looks nice. They have a mutual interest—swimming—and enjoy sharing the experience of playing together. But once we leave the pool, the friendship is left behind. The mutual interests no longer exist beyond the diving board and foam noodles.

As an adult, I've made those types of friends at work or as I've traveled. But unlike my daughter, I expect those relationships to stick. She knows that girl was her "pool friend" for the day and can walk away confident, knowing she had fun. It takes hard work, time, and repeated opportunities to develop and nurture the kind of friendships that stick. If I were to replace *friendships* in that last sentence with *hobbies* or *work*, I wouldn't hesitate to admit that I only have the capacity to focus on one or two areas at a time. But when it comes to friends, the world shouts that I should have more (and be great at making them by now), and I feel like a failure when I can only focus on digging deep with a few instead of investing in many.

God created us for relationships. We need friends—but maybe we don't need to make them, keep them, or have a certain number of them like "everyone else."

And making new friends as an adult isn't easy. Unlike how it was in high school or college, we simply don't have the same long-term shared experience (without the competition of the workplace or balancing the busy schedules of our families) to create the bonds that were so easy to form when we had fewer responsibilities—and were less picky about who we spent time with. Social media has given us the incredible opportunity to connect with far more people than ever before, but 90 percent of the people I enjoy following on Instagram would never show up to help us move, or babysit our daughter, or be invited to go on vacation or a double date with us.

I'd been working at my current ministry job for more than a year before I finally stopped waiting for coworkers to invite us for dinner and sent my own invitation. Once someone finally responded, it took another few weeks before we could find a day and time that worked for our families. And then a few more days to call in favors to find a babysitter, and a day or so when I wondered if we should just cancel and stay home. I was afraid that I wouldn't be good at social interactions outside of the office or small talk that didn't revolve around our kids. Should I be funny and entertaining? What if we didn't have anything in common other than our ministry? What if this fun attempt to be friends with my coworkers actually made it more awkward at work?

Ultimately, friendships are formed when we make the effort to put ourselves in situations where we can connect with people personally. That dinner was worth the effort to get together, and it was an encouraging reminder that people don't need us to entertain them—but they do want us to be good humans who care enough to be present. Although we didn't form any best friendships that evening, and we haven't found time to get together again, we did find a few new things we had in common.

> **Friendships are formed when we make the effort to put ourselves in situations where we can connect with people personally.**

When God created Adam and Eve, He knew it wasn't good for man to be alone (Genesis 2:18). God walked in that garden with them. He promises to be with us and sent His own Son to come to earth, to walk with us, eat with us, teach us, and love us as an example of what it looks like to be in community with one another.

I've always wanted to be popular. Long before social media taught us that "viral" could be a good thing and not an illness, I wanted *that*—to be known, included, invited, and part of a group of friends that would last a lifetime. When I was in elementary school, I thought the best way to make friends was by never showing weakness. So I claimed I'd read all the books and knew all the answers, and I didn't let those boys who chased me around the playground win. Later I thought the best way to make friends was by fitting in at all costs—which meant my beloved purple boots that I'd carefully circled in the JCPenney catalog were only worn once, because someone on the bus called them my "Barney boots."*

It took me far too long to discover that friendship isn't about being the best, but about being honest. The friendships I have now that have lasted through high school and college are with women who have seen me at my absolute worst. They've seen me fail in big ways. They've seen me grieve; they've been to my house when it was a mess; and we've survived seasons of hurt and distance and forgiveness. The friendships I tried to make to be popular weren't based on anything real. They were built on the understanding that I would look or act a certain way or on a fleeting shared experience that never had the chance to dig beneath the surface and find roots.

I wish I'd read Proverbs 18:24 in those early years of figuring out friendship: "There are 'friends' who destroy each other, but a real friend sticks closer than a brother" (NLT). Commentator Matthew Henry connects the "real friend" in this verse to Jesus. As he puts it, "Christ Jesus never will forsake those who trust in and love him. May we be such friends to others, for our Master's sake."[2]

Oh, the stories I could tell of feeling broken to pieces over

---

* For those of you who are not older than the Internet, Barney was a giant purple dinosaur on a popular kids' TV show. He danced and sang—and yes, it was weird, but not any stranger than what is on Netflix, so leave me alone, Karen.

friendships. I remember sitting on a panel at a conference one time, talking about friendship and community with women, while a friendship was breaking with a woman just a few seats away. God instructs us in His Word to choose friends wisely—not because we're to form exclusive cliques, but because the draw of popularity and numbers will be an opportunity for Satan to distract and destroy. When our hearts are hurt in a deep way by a friend, we carry that baggage with us into the next opportunity to make a friend. And we can find ourselves afraid to be real or to invest completely because our brains remind us of how badly it went last time, and our hearts—covered in scars and a little beat up—hold back.

In this world we may find ourselves thinking that we should have more friends or that the friends we do have should make our lives easier by sharing the load of cookouts and playdates and planning. We look around and see groups of women who seem to have it all together; we watch movies where a half dozen friends from college stick together as adults, and we think we should have been able to do that too. We feel guilty because we think we should find more time to spend with friends when we're in seasons that draw us deeply into parenting, marriage, work, and serving. I know it's not just me, because women share these stories and struggles with me all the time.

But what we really should do is lean into Jesus. He is the friend who will never disappoint us or leave us. We can't place those expectations on the women in our lives. But we can learn from Proverbs 18:24—and Jesus' own model—to embrace the few so we can experience more.

Jesus carefully selected His inner circle of three. He specifically invited the twelve apostles to join him. And then He obediently and lovingly spoke to the one, or ate with a few, or preached a sermon to thousands. When we swap the shout of should that tells us, "We need more," for Jesus' model to *dig deep with a few*, we can trade expectations for joy, insecurities for peace.

The women God has placed in your life, in this season—how can you invest more fully in them? Not by spending more time, or doing more activities, or having a bigger group, but by using the time you do have to be present, to invite, to listen, and to cheer for what God is doing in their lives? We won't feel left out when we're intentionally rooted right where God has us.

We won't feel left out when we're intentionally rooted right where God has us.

When we get to heaven, I don't think we'll be asked to prove how popular we were or how many friends we had. But did we love well the ones God gave us? Did the people in our lives come to know God because we cared more about their hearts than what they could do for us?

Imagine the legacy we'll leave for the generation behind us when we show them what it looks like to build healthy, beautiful friendships that form out of the overflow of hearts connected deeply to Jesus.

Digging Deeper

> Blessed is she who has believed that the Lord
> would fulfill what he has spoken to her!
>
> LUKE 1:45

When it comes to biblical examples of adult friendships, the story of Mary and Elizabeth is one of my favorites. Two cousins, chosen by

God for incredible tasks, who honored and supported each other with humility and love.

Here's the thing I love about the book of Luke. In his own words, Luke says that he "carefully investigated everything from the very first, to write to you in an orderly sequence" (1:3). This was a writer who carefully and strategically included each account of Jesus' life in Scripture, and the relationship between Mary and Elizabeth passed his litmus test.

Matthew starts his Gospel focused on Jesus' family tree and an angel of the Lord explaining what was happening to Joseph (1:1-25). Mark begins his Gospel well into the life of John the Baptist and Jesus, as John prepared the way for the Lord (1:1-8). John launches his Gospel (1:1-18) with poetic theology that refers back to the first words of Genesis: "In the beginning." Only Luke spends time recording the relationship between the two women who were chosen to carry John the Baptist and Jesus.

Elizabeth and Zechariah were an unlikely pair to be chosen as the parents of the man whom God would have "preparing for and announcing the coming of Jesus."[3] They were older and had never been able to have any children. Zechariah was a faithful priest, but not a significant religious leader. Still, they were "righteous in God's sight" (Luke 1:6). Even before Jesus came as our Savior, God was already showing us that it's not who we are, what our titles are, or how important we are that matters. What matters is that our lives reflect Him.

One miraculous conception down, one to go! Mary's story is familiar to us—a virgin visited by an angel and told that she will give birth to the Son of God. This happened six months after Elizabeth discovered that she was, in fact, pregnant. What a beautiful gift for God to choose these cousins and to use the good news of Elizabeth's pregnancy to comfort Mary when she questioned how her own could possibly happen. "Consider your relative Elizabeth," the angel Gabriel told her. "Even she has conceived a son in her old age, and this is the sixth month for her who was called childless. For nothing will be impossible with God" (Luke 1:36-37).

So Mary set off to be with Elizabeth—"hurried," in fact (verse 39)—to the only woman on the planet who could possibly understand what was happening. We don't see a lot of their interaction or their time together, but what we do see is a significant model of friendship that we can put into practice.

Mary and Elizabeth were both women who were chosen and favored by God. They were faithful and loved Him and believed that He could make the impossible possible. When Mary rushed into Elizabeth's house, Elizabeth—having waited far longer to finally experience this miracle—could have made it all about her. But instead, filled with the Holy Spirit, Elizabeth celebrated Mary and the baby she carried: "Blessed are you among women, and your child will be blessed! How could this happen to me, that the mother of my Lord should come to me? For you see, when the sound of your greeting reached my ears, the baby leaped for joy inside me. Blessed is she who has believed that the Lord would fulfill what he has spoken to her!" (Luke 1:42-45).

As for Mary, instead of making it all about *her*, which would have been reasonable considering she was carrying the Savior of the world, she turned the focus back to God in praise (verses 46-55).

These cousins, at different stages of life, came together with humility and love to support each other through an experience that no one else on earth could relate to, and they kept God at the center.

When we make our friendships about ourselves, our accomplishments, and what we can be praised for, we miss an opportunity to celebrate the women God has placed in our lives. And when our friends cheer for us and affirm what God is doing in our lives and we fail to place the praise back on Him, we miss an opportunity to give credit where it's due with a humble heart.

Is God bringing friendships to life for you right now for which you could use the "Do not be afraid" instruction the angel gave Zechariah and Mary (Luke 1:13,30)? Lean in to the friendships that you've been blessed with in this season—the ones that don't look like you think they should, the ones that are harder than you thought they would be, the ones that don't feel like enough in a world that says you should have many. And, like Mary, Elizabeth, and even Zechariah, use your words to praise God for His gifts and trust Him to make the impossible possible.

Flip the Script

- Flip "You should have a best friend" to "God, thank You for giving me a heart that includes more than just one person."

- Flip "You should be friends with everyone you meet" to "God, help me always be kind and thoughtful but also remember that You do not call me to be all things for all people."

- Flip "You should spend more time with your friends" to "God, this stage of life is beautiful and busy, and I'm grateful for grace in this season."

Reflection / Book Club

Friendships are hard, but we need them. We need women in our lives who will leap for joy when we share good news with them, and we need women whose examples will encourage us when we're not quite sure what God is doing in our lives. But in order to make room for healthy, God-centered relationships, we might need to let go of the baggage we carry with us from being burned in the past.

Be encouraged in knowing that you aren't alone in the struggle to make friends as an adult—but be excited, as well, as you trust that God isn't done with you yet. We are made for relationship with God and with one another!

1. Journal or share about your worst friendship experience. What made it so hard, and is there a part of it you're still struggling to leave in the past?

2. What expectations do you need to give up in order to make room for more joy in your relationships?

3. What impact would swapping insecurities for peace have on your friendships, and what would you need to do to make that exchange?

4. Assess honestly how open you are to inviting new friendships into your life or your current circle. What is it that keeps you from making more room for women in your life? (Maybe it's the fear that you'll be replaced or rejected?)

God, thank You for giving us examples of friendship in the Bible, but most of all thank You for giving us Jesus—the best friend we could ever have. Open our eyes and hearts to the women you want in our lives and help us honor You in every conversation as we release expectations and embrace the joy of simply loving others the way You love us. In Jesus' name, amen.

Quiet Time

A Woman Who Fears the Lord

Charm is deceptive and beauty is fleeting,
but a woman who fears the LORD will be praised.

PROVERBS 31:30

Read Proverbs 31:10-31

The original #bossmama, the unnamed woman in Proverbs 31, is typically touted as the gold standard for women. She works hard, provides for her family, never rolls her eyes when her kids ask her the same question for the hundredth time. Her clothes are handmade—today she would probably have a capsule wardrobe full of ethically made clothing and would know the names of the people who created everything she purchased. She is trustworthy and beloved, wise and strong.

If I didn't admire her, I think I'd dislike her. When we spend time comparing ourselves to other women online and in our real lives, our hearts can become hardened even against women in the Bible. In that case, the Proverbs 31 woman isn't viewed as someone to celebrate and emulate, but as a threat—someone who puts us on the defensive because we'll never measure up—instead of a model of love and generosity.

As you read today's passage, make note of where your brain reads the words but your heart hears "should." What has happened in your past—maybe long ago or as recently as a few minutes ago—to cause that reaction?

If you have time, choose a translation of Scripture you don't normally read, maybe the Amplified Bible or The Message—and read

Proverbs 31 again. Is there anything new that stands out now that you're able to read with fresh eyes or with a slightly more objective heart?

Quiet Quest

Today, set the timer on your phone for two minutes and leave it on the other side of the room. Sit in the quiet—no agenda, no rules, just space for you and God to connect (or reconnect if it's been a while).

Believe in the Lord

Believe in the Lord Jesus, and you will be saved.

ACTS 16:31

Read Acts 16:25-33

A few months ago, our house rumbled violently and unexpectedly. We live near an army base and will often hear loud booms or the low hum of a helicopter, but this was different. As one does, I immediately went to Facebook. After scrolling through the typical posts complaining about, well, everything, I found it. The official cause of our house rumble was an earthquake.

If we lived in California I might have understood, even expected it. But we live on the East Coast, where we signed up for blizzards, not earthquakes. Our homes aren't prepared for that kind of shaking, and our hearts certainly weren't prepared to hear our dishes rattle in the cabinets.

Imagine being the jailer in this chapter in Acts when an even more unexpected earthquake ripped through the prison walls and the cell doors banged open. Somehow, he slept through it all, and when he woke up, he was sure everyone had escaped. Instead, although Paul, Silas, and the other prisoners could have snuck past their deep-sleeping guard, they stayed—and the result was transformative. Immediately the jailer invited them to share the salvation message, and he believed, took the men and their message to his home, and—like Lydia and her family—his entire household believed and was baptized. The Christian Standard Bible says they were baptized "right away" (Acts 16:33). No turning back, no hesitating, no second-guessing.

Our influence over the people God has placed in our lives is more powerful than any earthquake. When our world feels shaken, we can stand firm, ready to share God's love with those who are finally waking up. And it might just change the lives of generations yet to come.

Quiet Quest

Grab a notebook or piece of paper and write about the last time your world felt shaken. Go into detail, answering all those key writing questions: Who? What? Where? When? Why? How? Ask God to show you where He was in the midst of the mess. How have you emerged stronger or changed? Whom can you stand with now who might be going through something similar?

God's Chosen Ones

As God's chosen ones, holy and dearly loved, put on
compassion, kindness, humility, gentleness, and patience.

COLOSSIANS 3:12

Read Colossians 3:12-13

I took a walk around the soccer field the other night. I was trying to escape the swarm of hardy bugs that were enjoying the hot summer night and hoped to clear my mind while burning a few calories. The more I walked, the more my mind raced—from to-do lists to upcoming events to random bursts of conversation with God about frustrating situations to what to have for dinner. I was so lost in the noise of all the thoughts that I nearly had a heart attack when a bunny jumped out of the woods near the path.

I knew most of what I wished God could fix for me were things that I'd said "yes" to without consulting Him. I was overwhelmed and feeling frazzled. Instead of intentionally putting on "compassion, kindness, humility, gentleness, and patience" (Colossians 3:12), I had chosen to start my days with a thick covering of crabbiness, fear, doubt, comparison, and pride. Choosing to listen to the shoulds had taken me out of a place of peace. Instead of enjoying a lovely walk at the park, I was fearing death by small, furry wildlife.

Where the world says we should hold grudges, be the best, say "yes" to all the things, and fight for what we deserve, a little time in God's Word will show us a different path. One that requires doing the hard work of forgiveness, staying humble, inviting others to participate in opportunities we don't need to take ourselves, and leaving the fight up to God. It's on that path, the narrow one, where we'll discover peace and joy as we quiet the shouts of should.

Quiet Quest

Whether it's in your living room, around the block, or at the local park, go for a walk today. No music in your headphones, no podcast to listen to, just yourself and your thoughts. Pray as you walk, sharing it all—the good, bad, messy, and confusing—with God. In what areas of your life have you put on something other than love lately?

Love Endures

[Love] bears all things, believes all things,
hopes all things, endures all things.

1 CORINTHIANS 13:7

Read 1 Corinthians 13:4-7

Love. We use the same word to talk about our affection for our spouse, our favorite drink from Starbucks, and the way we feel about God. There are dozens of ways we use one of the most important words—and actions—in our day-to-day lives. It's no wonder we struggle with feeling like we should be a better mom, wife, friend, sibling, and coworker. We know we're to love the people God has placed in our lives, but *how*? If I love someone less than my latte but more than my favorite shoes, is that good enough?

Today's scripture passage gives us a better understanding of what loving people well really looks like. If we're loving our new purse but are impatient, unkind, rude, and arrogant toward the people we live with, we're not loving at all.

Love bears all things—the unexpected project, the pile of shoes inside the front door, the worst of our family's actions.

Love believes—that God created us to be loyal, to believe in others and expect the best of them, and to be capable of more love than we could ever imagine.

Love hopes—even when the shoulds are the loudest, the doubts are the strongest, the hurts are the most painful.

Love endures—because the grace, mercy, and kindness we show others comes from the One who is love, not from a place of obligation.

Quiet Quest

As you think about some of the areas where you feel the shout of should the loudest in your life, consider how love could bring some quiet. Whom have you struggled to love lately? Reread today's scripture, knowing that what it describes is exactly how God loves you— and how you're called to love that difficult-to-get-along-with person. Rest there today.

The Hard Work

Do the hard work of getting along with each other,
treating each other with dignity and honor.

James 3:18 MSG

Read James 3:17-18

Over the course of my career I have been told to spend more time making friends and then told to spend less time socializing. I've been told that I should stop worrying so much about what everyone else is doing, and I've been reprimanded for blazing my own trail instead of following along. I have put myself out there to make friends with women I work with, only to watch the relationship crumble on an unsteady base of gossip and comparison. Is it any wonder I prefer to work at home?

For one of my former jobs, I traveled around the country as an MC for events that were focused on friendship. Today's verse was part of our core message, and even in the middle of those events, surrounded by cupcakes and confetti, talking about friendship was much easier than actually being a good friend. It's easy to talk about "being the friend you wish you had" and encouraging women to "just put yourself out there with one small, brave step." It's another thing to actually do the work.

Struggling to make or keep friends isn't something new. We can't blame it on social media or our busy lives when we see scripture that encourages us to "do the hard work of getting along" (James 3:18 MSG). It's not about putting on a mask and pretending to be someone you're not or listening to the shoulds that tell you friendship can only look a certain way or requires a certain number of people. Friendships, the kind that last, are built on the solid foundation of Jesus, where the overflow pours honor and dignity into the lives of those around us. It takes hard work, intentional time with God, and courage to commit to doing this well with just one other person.

Quiet Quest

When it comes to forming lasting friendships, who are the women in your life who have done this well? When you look at the friendships in your life right now, are there areas that need a little TLC or hard work? As you spend time with God today, ask Him for just one name of one woman who needs to be encouraged, honored, or included, and then commit to doing the hard work of consistently showing her grace and love. Commit to building up a community of women who can show the next generation how powerful friendship can be in God's kingdom.

Part 2

Personality and Possessions

4

I Should Have More Things by Now

I lived five minutes away from the King of Prussia Mall when I was in college. If you're unfamiliar with this East Coast phenomenon, it offers more than 400 stores to help you empty your wallet of all your hard-earned money. My roommate and I would drive over to enjoy our favorite ice cream for dinner, and my family loved visiting every time they made the two-hour trip to see me. I bought countless shirts that I absolutely had to own, Christmas gifts for friends and family, candles, and the makeup that the girl at the MAC counter said I *must* have.

With the exception of a few items my husband and I fell in love with at Crate and Barrel and added to our wedding registry, I own approximately zero of the things I bought at the mall while I was in college. The clothes definitely don't fit any more, and the accessories were sold long ago at a yard sale or have been replaced with something new. Where I should have been saving and paying off those student loans, I chose instead to embrace the rush of buying a new outfit or finding the perfect gift for a friend. And when I used my credit card to pay, I never felt the loss of that money—until the statement came a few weeks later, and I wondered how in the world I'd spent *that* much.

In Margo Aaron's article "Why We Buy Things We Don't Need," she explores how buying something is never really about the object, but about the emotional experience associated with the purchase. The outfit you buy, the gym membership you purchase, the new table you can't live without—you don't buy these things because they're required for your survival, but because you're looking for a "permission slip into a life you never dreamed possible for you." Our society has "set up a system where 'stuff' is a prerequisite for success," and most of us find ourselves not shopping out of necessity, but obligation, expectation, or competition.[1]

So what is it that draws us into Target, promising ourselves that this time we really will *just* buy the toothpaste, and brings us to the register with $50 worth of items we never knew we needed? What causes us to hold yard sales to clear out the clutter, only to replace the items we just sold within a few months? Or maybe you never let go of anything and find a sense of accomplishment in knowing that buying new things isn't an issue for you.

Our feelings around "stuff" come from pride, insecurity, and greed. Pride tells us that we're better than the women around us because we don't struggle in this way. Insecurity shouts at us that we'll never be a part of that group, get that job, be taken seriously if we don't dress a certain way or have that car or a certain size house. Greed silences our gratitude and keeps us from enjoying and appreciating what God has given us. We believe the lie that in order to do more, we have to have more. When we listen to the shoulds the world shouts at us, we're distracted from being the good stewards God has called us to be.

> **Greed silences our gratitude and keeps us from enjoying and appreciating what God has given us.**

American culture tells us that there are certain things we must have in order to become successful or to be considered a success. We want nicer homes, newer cars. We want to be able to hire someone to help with daily needs like housekeeping, landscaping, and personal training. We want to own the latest and greatest electronics. We want to take vacations![2]

Somewhere along the way, the things we own shifted away from the necessities to survive and became requirements to thrive. Unfortunately, when we set our eyes on the things of this world, we are bound for disappointment and discontentment. Writer Jeff Haden notes that "new always becomes the new normal… 'Things' provide only momentary bursts of happiness."[3] When we cling fast to material objects, we have no room to hold tight to Jesus.

In the book of Luke, Jesus shared this same truth with a crowd of thousands. After one man demanded that Jesus make his brother share their inheritance, Jesus said this:

> "Watch out and be on guard against all greed, because one's life is not in the abundance of his possessions." Then he told them a parable: "A rich man's land was very productive. He thought to himself, 'What should I do, since I don't have anywhere to store my crops? I will do this,' he said.

'I'll tear down my barns and build bigger ones and store all my grain and my goods there. Then I'll say to myself, "You have many goods stored up for many years. Take it easy; eat, drink, and enjoy yourself." ' But God said to him, 'You fool! This very night your life is demanded of you. And the things you have prepared—whose will they be?' That's how it is with the one who stores up treasure for himself and is not rich toward God" (Luke 12:15-21).

What is the bigger barn you're trying to build? Is it a career, house, car, vacation, or the latest technology? All the things you've gathered around yourself—the stuff you refuse to part with because you might need it someday or because it makes you feel superior in your thriftiness—what will that do for you at the end of your life?

> **When we cling fast to material objects, we have no room to hold tight to Jesus.**

The things we own and the dreams we have aren't good or bad on their own. Money, as has often been said, is morally neutral—it's our attitudes about it that become the problem. The same is true with our possessions. A house can't be bad, but our attitude—our discontentment or our pride—can become a problem when we become focused on it and forget to give thanks to the One who gives it to us.

Contentment isn't just about wanting less, but about doing more to honor God with the things we already have.

My husband and I come from very different backgrounds regarding finances and material possessions. He is frugal, financially savvy, and plans for the future. I enjoy a good "treat yourself" moment, am always looking for the next new thing, and love making memories in the present instead of saving for some unknown date in the future. We're a good team—but some of our more deeply rooted habits and feelings about money and "stuff" have led to some hard conversations to navigate.

When I was growing up, shopping was a way to escape. A trip to the mall with my mom worked the same way as an escape into a good book. Looking for a cute shirt meant I didn't have to think about what was happening at school or home. It was also a way to spend quality time with my mom and sister when going to the local mall was really the only activity available on a weekend for our small town. I knew absolutely nothing about my family's finances and assumed everything was fine because no one was telling me otherwise. We went on vacations, stocked up on craft supplies at AC Moore, and said "yes" to high school trips to England, Scotland, and Disney World (times two, as my twin sister did all those activities as well).

My husband, on the other hand, grew up with hand-me-downs and yard sales and knew far more about the state of his family's finances at a young age than I might even know now as an adult. Whereas I chose my college because of its prestigious name and potential career opportunities, he chose his based on closeness to family and tuition price. I enjoyed living on campus and having the full college experience with friends, while he worked at least one job, sometimes more, the entire time so he wouldn't be majorly in debt after graduation. I focused on the fun of right now, while he planned frugally for the future—our future.

Our marriage has matured into a beautiful balancing act. His saving has allowed us to enjoy a home, new cars, and a solid retirement plan. My "in the moment" living has encouraged him to enjoy spontaneous trips, take our daughter on adventures, and give to those in need. Together we have said "yes" to some things he may not have experienced as a kid, as our daughter plays soccer and we go to baseball games. And we've also said "no" to some things that I would have experienced as a kid, like buying a new item when we had something similar that still worked or having our daughter participate in all the activities, regardless of cost.

There is a house down the road from us that I've had my eye on for a year. It's beautiful, has the perfect floor plan, is in a little community we love, and far exceeds our budget. I struggle to appreciate what we have now when I drive past what could be.

My husband loves the idea of a yard sale but struggles to let go of things. As I set up the tables and put price stickers on items that we haven't used in years to create a less cluttered space and save for a future vacation, he wanders around, reclaiming items we should keep "just in case."

It's a balancing act with give and take, ups and downs. Sometimes we do it well, and other times I come home with new shoes and my husband holds on to old papers and greeting cards. We're a work in progress.

But we're learning to swap clutter for creativity as we quiet the shout of should about our possessions. We don't need something new; we just need to find new ways to use what we already have. We don't need a bigger house; we just need to be creative as we move furniture around. We don't need to go on a fancy vacation every year; we just need to take the time to discover the adventures in our own backyard.

Swapping clutter for creativity is worth the hard work when it makes our homes feel peaceful and our time together more enjoyable. We can savor the life God has given us while also being good stewards of our needs for today and our dreams for tomorrow.

Digging Deeper

> All these people have put in gifts out of their surplus, but
> she out of her poverty has put in all she had to live on.
>
> LUKE 21:4

I love reading through the parables that Jesus tells in the New Testament because they remind me that God knows where we struggle and was gracious to share His wisdom with us. From managing anxiety and worry to loving our neighbors and living generously, the parables Jesus shared weren't just for the disciples or the crowds who were with Him, but for us.

It might be easy to read those sections of Luke and think that Jesus simply hates when we shop or don't invest our money or don't give enough. But when we understand who Jesus is and what He's really saying in these chapters, we'll come to realize that what God really desires isn't a significant return on investment for our salvation, but a full, deep, committed relationship.

In Luke 19:45 Jesus arrives in Jerusalem, having just made His "triumphal entry" into the city. The temple, which should have been a place for prayer and worship—for God's people to come and be with Him—had turned into an ancient version of the King of Prussia Mall. Jesus wasn't in the habit of throwing shop owners out of their own places of business, but when it came to using this holy place in a way that distracted people from the true purpose of their time with God, Jesus wasn't having it.

Matthew 21:12 says, "Jesus went into the temple and threw out all those buying and selling. He overturned the tables of the money changers and the chairs of those selling doves." It wasn't the people Jesus was attacking—He loves people. What He attacked was a religious system that had made the place of God about themselves. When the things we own and the stuff we just have to have shift our faith from a personal relationship with Jesus to personal gain for ourselves, we need Jesus to come in and toss out what doesn't belong. The world shouts that we should have more, while God whispers, "Just be with Me."

When it comes to the things we own or want or have on our vision boards, how much are we willing to give back to God? Are we generous out of our surplus (of time, talents, finances, or hospitality), or do we give all that we have, every little bit, to honor God and grow His kingdom? Do we trust God with all we have, or do we hold some back "just in case"?

In the verse following today's passage of Scripture (Luke 21:5), there's talk about how beautiful the temple looks, which is in stark contrast to what matters most to Jesus. Humans place value on the outside—the shiny exterior, the way something looks and stands out and is the fanciest—while what God cares about is what's inside. He does not care about the impressive things we've collected, but rather what is happening inside us. Have we adorned our lives with things that impress the world, or are we quietly and humbly giving our hearts fully to God? Do we care more about what He sees in us than what our neighbors or coworkers or family see on the outside?

As we seek to quiet the clutter in our lives, we can create space for

God to move in our hearts, leaving a legacy for our families that will last far longer than any "thing" ever would.

Flip the Script

- Flip "You should buy the newest phone" to "God, today I'm grateful for what I already have and know that it's more than enough."

- Flip "You should want a new house or a fancier car to show others you're successful" to "God, help me remember that my success isn't dependent on my possessions, but on how I serve You."

- Flip "You should use credit cards to pay for what you want, even if you can't afford it" to "God, I want to be a good steward of the resources You give me, even if it means having less."

Reflection / Book Club

This isn't an easy balance to strike—to experience a life that is full of creativity and joy and generosity while also being responsible stewards of what God has given us. But we worship a God who knows every obstacle we'll ever face, every struggle, doubt, disappointment, and fear—and He's there to walk with us every step of the way. We can turn to His Word for guidance, find peace as we seek His wisdom through prayer, and receive support and encouragement through the community He's given us as we surround ourselves with people who love us more than the things we own.

1. As you think about your relationship with "things," are your decisions typically driven out of pride, insecurity, or greed?

2. How could living more creatively help to clear the clutter—whether your mind is cluttered with a growing list of things you think you should have or your house is cluttered with things you think you should keep?

3. When have you made a purchase based on the expectations of others or to achieve what you viewed as "success"?

4. Spend some time in prayer today, quieting the world's shout of should so you can lean into the peaceful presence of Jesus. Consider these questions: What can you let go of to make room for God to work deeper in your life? Where have you been holding back from giving back to God what He's given to you?

> *Father, thank You for valuing what's on the inside over what we see on the outside. Help us want more of You in our lives and less of things that won't last. May all that we have, all the gifts that You've given us, be used for Your kingdom and not to build our own. We trust You and we love You. In Jesus' name, amen.*

I Should Want to Host

As we kayaked around the lake a few days ago, I asked my daughter what she had on her bucket list for the rest of the summer. We had just returned from an overnight trip with family and a baseball game with friends, and we were heading into a week full of swimming lessons, soccer practices, and art projects. I knew she was a kid after my own heart when she gave me a few answers and all of them included the phrase "with just our family." Just the three of us. No huge crowds, no extra friends—just our little family, focused on one another. *Hi, we're the Stine family, and we're all introverts.*

But while we have a desire—and sometimes a physical need—to stay at home without any extra people, the world shouts that we should love hospitality. We should have people over to our house all the time. Our door should always be open to have all the people over for all the things.

In the same way that God has uniquely created each of us to work and rest (a topic I dive deep into in my book *Holy Hustle*), I believe He has also created each of us to be unique in how we approach hospitality. What does it look like to obediently use the spaces God has given us to honor Him and love others without burning ourselves out or stretching ourselves too thin?

Hospitality has been a big topic lately, as countless books—in both secular and Christian circles—tell us what it should look like, and stores sell us on what we should have in order to do it well. Can we host if we don't own linen napkins, string twinkly lights outside, or grow peonies? All the expectations we feel as we see or read about what others are doing are shoulds we carry with us, but they aren't the heart of hospitality. When we swap the obligation the world shouts at us (to host everyone well, all the time) for the invitation God gives us (to love people well), we'll discover that we can also swap fear for freedom.

> When we swap obligation for invitation,
> we can also swap fear for freedom.

Consider Thanksgiving. Days spent preparing menus and shopping in crazy, crowded grocery stores. Hours spent cleaning, moving furniture, and finding the nice plates you just had to have at your wedding—only to realize they do more dust collecting than food serving. At some point over the last few years everyone in your family has started to come to your home for Thanksgiving, and now it's "tradition." A tradition that causes you to lose sleep, panic about a turkey at 5:00 a.m., and wonder if this will finally be the year Aunt Mildred finds something nice to say.

When people start to show up, dressed in their cutest Thanksgiving outfits and talking excitedly about the parade, or the dog show, or the football game (none of which you got to watch), you hope the steam from the stovetop will help you look fresh and glowing, instead of sweaty and wilted. After hours of cooking and cleaning, you sit down to eat with your family—and in 20 minutes, it's over. You think back to other times you've hosted, the work and energy and time you invested only to have the food eaten or the conversation done in a flash. It's a cycle you're not sure is worth it: you prepare, work, and serve—and they come, eat, and leave. And Aunt Mildred still hasn't found anything nice to say.

Is this really what hospitality is supposed to look like? Begrudgingly hosting and hoping for a different outcome every time? In our current era of Airbnb and public five-star ratings for staying at someone's home, the pressure to be an outstanding host is overwhelming. Maybe a few of these questions are going through your head:

- *How do I do this if I don't have a second home to rent out or even a second bedroom to offer to an overnight guest?*

- *How can I be a good host as an introvert?*

- *How can I make guests feel welcomed without falling into the cycle of needing more "things"?*

- *I'm tired of being the host. Shouldn't it be someone else's turn?*

We can rest easy knowing that the obligations we feel based on the shoulds the world shouts at us can be quieted. Consider 1 Peter 4:8-11.

> Above all, maintain constant love for one another, since love covers a multitude of sins. Be hospitable to one

another without complaining. Just as each one has received a gift, use it to serve others, as good stewards of the varied grace of God. If anyone speaks, let it be as one who speaks God's words; if anyone serves, let it be from the strength God provides, so that God may be glorified through Jesus Christ in everything.

As Christians we can be friendly and generous to the people God brings into our lives while using the gifts God has given us to honor Him in each of our interactions. Let's remove the mental obstacles around hospitality by rethinking what it "should" look like. Loving others isn't something that has to happen through inviting others to our homes every weekend; it's something we can practice as we welcome coworkers into our office, sit with friends at swimming lessons, volunteer to serve those in need in our communities, or simply share what God has given us with just one person He has put in our lives. We don't need to spend money to be good at hospitality; we can be great hosts simply by loving others.

> We don't need to spend money to be good at hospitality; we can be great hosts simply by loving others.

However, unless we understand why hospitality is important, we'll always assume it's something other people do, or we'll find excuses to avoid it. Using our personalities, fears, busy schedules, or lack of resources, we'll find ways to convince ourselves that we don't have time or energy to put into inviting others into our lives. So what does hospitality do? Hospitality...

- keeps us connected to one another: "In Christ we, though many, form one body, and each member belongs to all the others" (Romans 12:5 NIV).

- gives us the opportunity to love our neighbors: "Love your neighbor as yourself" (Mark 12:31 NIV).

- keeps our hearts and eyes aware of the people around us who might need an invitation: "The next time you put on a dinner, don't just invite your friends and family and rich neighbors, the kind of people who will return the favor. Invite some people who never get invited out, the misfits from the wrong side of the tracks. You'll be—and experience—a blessing. They won't be able to return the favor, but the favor will be returned—oh, how it will be returned!—at the resurrection of God's people" (Luke 14:12-14 MSG).

- gives us the chance to give—and receive—encouragement: "Let us watch out for one another to provoke love and good works, not neglecting to gather together, as some are in the habit of doing, but encouraging each other, and all the more as you see the day approaching" (Hebrews 10:24-25).

- allows us and our guests the chance to use the gifts God has given us: "Just as each one has received a gift, use it to serve others, as good stewards of the varied grace of God" (1 Peter 4:10).

- opens the door for opportunities to build relationships and live out the Great Commission: "Go, therefore, and make disciples of all nations, baptizing them in the name of the Father and of the Son and of the Holy Spirit, teaching them to observe everything I have commanded you" (Matthew 28:19-20).

Which one of those will be your *why* the next time you make excuses that hospitality simply isn't your gift? Sure, some of us will find it easier to invite someone new into our lives or to host large gatherings. But hospitality isn't about the number of people you have in your home; it's about the way you love the people whose path God is crossing with yours. The beautiful gift that comes from quieting this shout of should means that we can make an exchange. We can swap fear (that we're not cut out to be a five-star hostess) for the freedom of honoring the friends, family, neighbors, and strangers God puts in our lives. And we make that swap by using the gifts God has given us. When we approach hospitality with this mindset, we won't be caught up in whether or not we're the only one offering the invitation. Instead, we'll be grateful for the opportunity to use our gifts to love others and introduce them to the Jesus we know and love.

Above a small garage there is a loft that was built just to host guests. In this space I learned more about hosting others well than at any hotel, resort, or vacation home I've ever visited. There is a key kept in a little mailbox by the back door of the home, with a note that informs the guest that absolutely no payment will be accepted (although gifts are usually placed in that mailbox as a small token of appreciation). Up the stairs and above the garage sits a beautiful room, just large enough for a sofa, coffee table, and one of the most comfortable beds I've ever slept on. There are snacks purchased from the grocery store down the road because Ms. Jean knows her strengths, and her strengths are not baked goods. The other half of the space offers a whirlpool tub in a private bathroom area. You won't find a TV or Wi-Fi inside, but outside you'll find a stunning garden—and an invitation to come, rest, and enjoy.

I'd never met anyone who had intentionally designed a home for other people as much as for themselves. Guest rooms and pull-out sofas, of course, but nothing like this—and with no expectation of anything in return.

Ms. Jean and her husband, Mr. Phil, have used what God has given them to offer a unique kind of hospitality right in the middle of our small town. Where most people build privacy fences, they have open doors. It's not elaborate or showy, and if you choose you could spend your entire time there without having to speak to anyone else. But the love, kindness, and joy they have put into using their home invites people to discover the quiet voice of God over the shouts of the world. And it's a legacy their children have inherited, as their son and daughter-in-law offer their beach home to guests who need some time away. This is a family with titles like accountant, teacher, financial adviser, runner, mom, dad, and grandparent, using the gifts God has given them to create comfortable, beautiful spaces for others to enjoy.

It's something my husband and I hope to model one day, to create that same kind of space for couples and creatives and guests to come and rest—but in our own way and in God's timing. Because you never leave Ms. Jean and Mr. Phil's guesthouse feeling like you were an obligation or a burden, but with a renewed spirit, a quiet heart, and an appreciation for the kind of hospitality that invites you to simply say "yes" to the invitation.

As I look around our home, I see all the reasons why we shouldn't be able to do this right now. We don't have space for guests because our rooms are full of Legos and art supplies. As much as we love our backyard, it's a constant work in progress that currently has a four-foot unicorn sprinkler in the middle of it. We own only one set of amazing sheets and have no other bed to put them on.

There are so many excuses I could find, so many times I've been frustrated when it feels like we don't get together with friends if we're not the ones doing the inviting. But what if we stopped waiting for the perfect timing, the perfect home, the perfect balance of inviting and being invited? We don't look back on our time at Ms. Jean's and think about the spotless floors or regret going because the muffins were store bought. We enjoyed it because someone made room in their lives for us and cared enough to invite us in. Maybe there is someone in your life who needs to know that you love them more than you love a perfectly clean house.

This shift—from obligation to invitation—has helped me find the joy in hosting. In this season our home is perfect for welcoming other families who have young children, and none of the things we own are too precious for them to enjoy. That work-in-progress backyard is safe and peaceful—a great place to sit around a fire with friends or watch the kids play in the unicorn sprinkler. Instead of trying to feed everyone ourselves, we host potlucks so each family has the food they know their kids will actually eat (ours likes sushi; some prefer hot dogs). It's a reminder to look at each season and ask God to show us how we can practice practical, imperfect, God-honoring hospitality for the people He has put in our lives.

How can we create a safe space for others to come and quiet their hearts in a place where they feel welcomed and wanted? That kind of hospitality doesn't require a big house, fancy food, or an eye for interior design—just a heart willing to share what we have and who we are with someone else.

Digging Deeper

> Now please swear to me by the LORD that
> you will also show kindness to my father's
> family, because I showed kindness to you.
>
> JOSHUA 2:12

The book of Joshua details what happens to the Israelites after Moses died. After wandering in the desert for 40 years, the new generation of Israelites is now allowed to enter the land God had promised them. It's a beautiful story of God's faithfulness in keeping His covenant.

Joshua is preparing the people to cross the Jordan and claim the land God has promised them. They're gathering their belongings, spreading the word, and getting ready to move. As they do this, Joshua sends two spies into the land to scout and report back so they know what they're about to face—specifically in the city of Jericho. Why Jericho? It wasn't just a city; it was a fortress. By conquering this place, the Israelites would find security and safety, while also putting themselves right in the middle of the Canaanites' communication plans and supply routes. God has promised Joshua the victory, but He hasn't detailed the exact plan. So, as a seasoned military leader, Joshua uses his experience and knowledge, plus his faith that God will do what He says, to set his people up for success.

This is where Rahab the prostitute comes in. The two spies have to stay somewhere when they arrive in Jericho, and a brothel is perhaps the one place these men could hope to remain undetected. But Rahab doesn't simply welcome strangers into her home—she puts her own life on the line. When the king sends men to ask her to turn over the spies (Joshua 2:3), she points them in the opposite direction—a move that, if discovered, could cost her life. But Rahab has faith that God will deliver her, and these spies will stay true to their word. She has heard what God has already done and about the victory He has given the Israelites, and instead of fearing the people who were about to come invade the city, Rahab begins to trust and fear the Lord.

When the Israelites attack the city, only Rahab and her family are set apart to be spared. Joshua sends the two spies back to her house where they escort her, and all who are in the house with her, to safety (6:22).

By opening the door of her home, Rahab stepped into the story God was writing for her life. One where she would no longer be known by her profession, but by a life marked by God's grace and faithfulness. A welcome into an inn and a scarlet cord saved Rahab's life (2:17-21), which eventually led to a closed inn and the birth of Jesus, who would save us all.

Rahab's story is a reminder that the label the world puts on us does not exclude us from playing a part in God's kingdom. But it also shows what can happen when we follow God—even when it means going against what others think we should do, or when what we do looks strange, or costs us something, or places us outside our comfort zone.

In the sixth book of the Bible we meet Rahab, and her identity is "prostitute" (Joshua 2:1), but that's not the end of her story. In the New Testament she is referred to as faithful (Hebrews 11:31), righteous (James 2:23-25), and an ancestor of Jesus (Matthew 1:5-6). What we do now does not determine the destiny God has for us. If we're willing, like Rahab, to step into the life God has prepared for us, the identity and shoulds the world puts on our shoulders will be exchanged for the truth that we are, ultimately, daughters of the King. And He has good work for us to do in His name.

The size of your home, where you live, the amount of free time or money you have, all the reasons you think you can't or shouldn't contribute to growing God's kingdom through hospitality—none of that matters. Follow Rahab's example. Love people well—and let God use the messy, imperfect parts of your life to bring hope to someone who needs to know they aren't alone. You never know where your story will go when you trust God to write it well.

> You never know where your story will go
> when you trust God to write it well.

Flip the Script

- Flip "You should have people over more often" to "God, thank You for my community and for the friends who love me just as I am."

- Flip "You should make sure everyone gets what they want every time they come over" to "God, I love being with my friends and family because of the memories we make, not the things we get."

- Flip "You should have the perfect home before you invite people over" to "God, thank You for not expecting me to be perfect before I can serve You."

Reflection / Book Club

Hospitality is about how we treat people, not about what we own, serve, or offer, which means you won't find this section wrapped up with "five simple solutions for biblical hospitality." Instead, let's look at some examples in Scripture and see what God has to say. Let's give Him the space to work in and through us, changing our hearts to be more like His in the way only He can. Grab your Bible and a journal and write out each of these verses:

- Hebrews 13:2

- 1 Peter 4:9

- Romans 12:13

- Titus 1:8

- Matthew 25:35

- 1 Peter 4:10

- Galatians 6:10

- Galatians 5:13

If one stands out to you, take some time to dig deeper. Read the entire chapter to understand the context. Read the introduction to that book of the Bible to discover when it was written, who wrote it, and what the major themes are. Spend some time in prayer, asking God to help you understand His Word and thanking Him for the opportunity to put your faith into action. Then, over the next week, stay alert. Watch for the people in your everyday, real life that you can love well— not as the perfect host, but as a friend.

1. Is hospitality something that comes naturally to you? What small, practical, God-focused piece of advice would you share with a friend to encourage them in this area?

2. How does your frustration about being the only one who ever hosts go away as you consider the role God is asking you to play in His kingdom? Or, if that's not something you struggle with, what blessings have you seen as a result of hosting others, even when it might not be convenient or easy?

3. Who in your life has been an example of hospitality? How have they inspired you?

Heavenly Father, thank You for inviting us to participate in growing Your kingdom and never expecting us to do it perfectly. As we seek to swap obligation for invitation and fear for freedom, help us listen to Your voice and not the overwhelming shouts of the world. May our doors be open to the people You've planned to bring into our lives, and may our hearts be open to receive all that You have for us. In Jesus' name, amen.

6

I Should Speak Up More/Less

Two women are sitting in the coffee shop you've just entered, both lost in thought. On the outside they couldn't be more different. One is dressed in bright, bold colors and sitting front and center at the counter, while the other is shyly sitting in the farthest corner, her soft, dark sweater wrapped tightly around her as she holds her drink. But they're both reflecting on recent conversations that were, surprisingly, similar.

The bold one just left a work meeting where she was told—again—that her excitement, confidence to speak her mind, and loud conversations she had with coworkers were distracting and discouraged. She was told—again—that she should be humble and quiet, and she is trying to figure out how to be someone she's not.

The shy one just left a work meeting where she was told—again—that her quiet demeanor and difficulty interacting with her coworkers were making her appear disinterested and standoffish. She was told—again—that she should be louder and more outgoing to prove that she valued her work and the people around her.

Two women. Bold and shy. Wondering how to navigate a world that shouts that we need to fix ourselves when all we want is to be ourselves, just as God made us.

The world celebrates "extra" and gives us models that show us what can happen when we put ourselves out there. If we're willing to be the biggest, loudest, most dramatic, and the squeakiest wheel, we'll find success. Doors will open! People will love us! But we also hear that we should stay humble, make sure we're not hurting anyone's feelings by sharing our success, and just quietly get our work done if we want to keep our jobs or receive future opportunities.

So which is it? Should we speak up more or speak less? Should we embrace who we are or stock up on a variety of masks to wear for each situation? This comes down to knowing God intimately so we can know who He created us to be. As much as our bosses, faith leaders, the media, and even family members want to tell us who we should be and what we should do in order to live our best life, we'll always be disappointing to someone who has different expectations. We receive criticism from others and even from our own thoughts, and the only way to swap criticism for confidence is to remember who made us and spend time with Him, allowing Him to mature us.

Maybe, like me, you remember specific situations in your life that have caused you to feel uncomfortable in your own skin. As a little girl I remember being shy and quiet, and I had a father who thought that combination meant I was being rude to people. I have more memories of being told to watch where I was going, to pay attention to other people, to speak up—but not too much. Value and emphasis were placed on how other people were treated, even strangers, and my own personality was trampled under the expectations of what I should be doing or saying.

Perhaps as you grew up and tried to develop your own voice, you were labeled a "princess" if your opinion went against what everyone else was thinking or doing. Instead of being encouraged to share your thoughts and feelings in productive, meaningful ways, you were told that you were high maintenance, dramatic, or unreasonable. Later in life you found yourself working for a boss who pushed you to do more, speak up, lead meetings, and voice your opinions—but only as long as it didn't cause tension or drama with anyone else. And when it did? You were told to be less and to work harder at being a team player, and you were expected to somehow do the same quality and quantity of work but with the added pressure to include/please everyone (with no coaching or training on how to do that).

In a *Time* article, author and researcher Deborah Tannen says, "When they talk in a formal setting, many women try to take up less verbal space by being more succinct, speaking in a lower voice and speaking in a more tentative way… If they talk in ways associated with authority, they can be seen as too aggressive… But if they don't—if they hold back in these and other ways—they risk being underestimated."[1]

It's a tension that many of us feel every day as we try to do what is expected of us at our job, switch to a different expectation at home, and maybe even switch to another to meet new friends or take our next step toward our dreams. When we look to Scripture to learn what God has to say about all of this, we don't find any hard and fast rules about how much or little women should speak, but we do find instructions for everyone regarding the best use of our words.

- "May the words of my mouth and the meditation of my heart be acceptable to you, LORD, my rock and my Redeemer" (Psalm 19:14).

- "LORD, set up a guard for my mouth; keep watch at the door of my lips" (Psalm 141:3).

- "There is one who speaks rashly, like a piercing sword; but the tongue of the wise brings healing" (Proverbs 12:18).

- "Pleasant words are a honeycomb: sweet to the taste and health to the body" (Proverbs 16:24).

- "Death and life are in the power of the tongue, and those who love it will eat its fruit" (Proverbs 18:21).

- "Her mouth speaks wisdom, and loving instruction is on her tongue" (Proverbs 31:26).

- "I tell you that on the day of judgment people will have to account for every careless word they speak" (Matthew 12:36).

- "It is with your heart that you believe and are justified, and it is with your mouth that you profess your faith and are saved" (Romans 10:10 NIV).

- "No foul language should come from your mouth, but only what is good for building up someone in need, so that it gives grace to those who hear" (Ephesians 4:29).

- "Let your speech always be gracious, seasoned with salt, so that you may know how you should answer each person" (Colossians 4:6).

- "My dear brothers and sisters, understand this: Everyone should be quick to listen, slow to speak, and slow to anger" (James 1:19).

- "Be doers of the word and not hearers only, deceiving yourselves" (James 1:22).

God, who created the entire world with His words, has given us a responsibility to use our words well. He has also created in each of us a unique personality through which we can communicate those words, and He has given us places and opportunities to use our words to bring glory to Him. If we allow the criticism of the world to keep us from having the confidence to express ourselves the way God intended, we might miss the chance to share the good news of the gospel with someone who needs to hear it. Confidence doesn't mean saying more, but rather being more intentional with the words we say.

Whether we speak more or speak less, it's not the quantity of our words that matters, but the quality. Are we using our words to build up others, to point them to God, and to bring healing? That can be done in three words, "I forgive you," or in fifty thousand words as we write the book God has put on our hearts. Or are we using our words to tear down, build our personal kingdoms, and hurt people?

Confidence doesn't mean saying more, but rather being more intentional with the words we say.

Let's be women who speak up—not because it's expected or encouraged, but because we have something to say that will change someone's life.

———

"Here is a list of the things you can and can't share online while you work for us." It was my first ministry job, and I was excited to start using my gifts with an organization I admired. I'd signed all the paperwork and set up my office, and all the new ideas were running through my mind. I'd gone through several rounds of complicated interviews, been a longtime supporter of the organization, and thought I knew what I was getting into. But I was also heading into this new role with a lot of baggage. I'd been hurt and disappointed after losing another job I'd loved and was flat-out grateful that anyone else would consider hiring me. I was willing to do whatever they asked to make sure they liked me, hired me, and kept me.

So I took their conservative list of online dos and don'ts, convinced myself that hiding parts of who I was and what I enjoyed was fine, and went all in. Every comment, thought, and photo was carefully considered to make sure I wasn't breaking any of the rules. In meetings I paid attention to the way everyone else talked, the Christian phrases they used, and the way they prayed, and I adopted it all into my own life. It didn't feel right to hide parts of my personality and the things I enjoyed, but it was written into my contract—and I'm nothing if not a rule follower.

But instead of working in ministry and growing deeper in my relationship with God, I found myself feeling lost, confused, and frustrated. I was doing and saying all the expected things, but I was still overlooked and left out. I had done incredible work and offered ideas that moved the ministry forward, and it wasn't enough. *I* wasn't enough. When I would voice an opinion that went against the bigger personalities in the group, it was either ignored, dismissed, or talked about (and then dismissed) in meetings after the meeting.

You can only wear a mask so long before you start to feel like you're suffocating. I grew resentful, anxious, envious, and angry. It was exhausting to present a perfect personality to the world while I was crumbling on the inside. I didn't understand how being myself wasn't good enough—especially in ministry—and eventually my relationships at work and my relationship with God all began to slip away. What I did and said and shared was never going to meet their standards, and I assumed that meant God had better things to do than listen to me.

When we focus on not being too much or too little, we lose who God made us to be. Satan knew exactly where the cracks were forming in me and, like the sneak that he is, took the small frustrations and doubts and magnified them until I lost everything. I might have had baggage with me when I started the job, but I left broken, buried, and bruised under the weight of failed expectations. It took years of counseling, rest, and prayer to find my way back, to finally look in the mirror and recognize the woman on the other side.

When we focus on not being too much or too little, we lose who God made us to be.

My fear of being worthless pushed me to put on whatever mask I needed to fit in, while inside I was conflicted because I also value authenticity. My desire to be considered worthwhile, just by being myself, wasn't met in a role where I was told to hide parts of who I was from the world. What I needed was for someone to say that I was loved simply for being myself, but what I was hearing was that being myself wasn't good enough. I could only work my way into so much affirmation and encouragement, and no amount of impressive tasks accomplished could fulfill what I didn't know I needed—someone to speak life into my heart by inviting me to simply be *me*.

Our words have power. And when we give someone the opportunity to share their voice, to use their words in the way God created them to be used, we build them up, celebrate our differences, and stay focused on the big picture. By embracing and sharing who we are—who God made us to be—online and in real life, we invite other women into a place where they feel safe to do the same. It's imperfect and messy and not always what we would expect, but if it honors God and brings Him glory, it's welcome here.

Digging Deeper

> Now may the God of hope fill you with all joy
> and peace as you believe so that you may overflow
> with hope by the power of the Holy Spirit.
>
> ROMANS 15:13

What if we could learn to use our words—regardless of how many we speak, how often, or how loudly—to become women of influence? Contrary to what the world may shout at us, having influence doesn't require having hundreds of thousands of followers online, employees who work for us, or a specific personality type. As the executive pastor at my church likes to say, "Leadership and influence are simply helping people move from here to there." You have influence over your family, friends, neighbors, community, coworkers, and anyone God has chosen to place in your life, and with it comes a responsibility to choose wisely the words you use as you interact with them.

The book of Romans in the New Testament contains simple and profound explanations of God's plan of salvation, love, mercy, grace, and forgiveness. The words Paul chose to share with the Romans are as relevant and powerful today as they were around AD 57. Our words, when used intentionally and with the purpose of growing God's kingdom, can leave a lasting impact.

Leading up to Romans 15, Paul tells the recipients of his letter (which now includes us) to stop being so judgy and not let their differences get in the way of their spiritual growth (Romans 14:1-12). He also instructs the Roman believers to "pursue what promotes peace and what builds up one another" (verse 19). With influence—which we all have as Christians—comes a responsibility to use our words to bring hope, healing, forgiveness, and the message of salvation. No one will come to know God's love through our judgment, criticism, gossip, or boasting in our own achievements.

In order to become women of influence, we need to be intentional about our words and humble in our approach. Paul could have used these final passages of his letter to remind the early believers of his importance and how closely he worked with Jesus. Instead, he shares, "I have reason to boast in Christ Jesus regarding what pertains to God. For I would not dare say anything except what Christ has accomplished through me by word and deed for the obedience of the Gentiles, by the power of miraculous signs and wonders, and by the power of God's Spirit" (Romans 15:17-19).

Are we sharing only what God has done through us, or are we using our words to boast about our own accomplishments? Are we taking the credit and inviting others to follow along, or are we giving Jesus the credit and inviting others to follow Him?

Paul reminds us to instill confidence in others by sharing not only truth, but truth with love. He tells us to give credit to Jesus and glory to God, inviting others into our lives to see that we don't have it all together while pointing to the hope we have in the One who does. And he charges us to take others from here to there by encouraging the gifts we see in them.

Paul may not have been able to be with the Romans personally, but he knew that if the good news of the gospel were to spread further in their community, it would be up to the believers to multiply the missionary work Paul was doing. He affirmed and encouraged them, pointing out that they had the knowledge they needed and the ability required to teach one another (Romans 15:14).

Our words, when used well, can invite others to take their next step on the path God has prepared for them. When we focus on the quality and purpose of our words instead of the quantity, our influence multiplies as we encourage someone else to use their gifts to bring honor and glory to God—and they then encourage someone else to do the same.

Flip the Script

- Flip "You should stand up for yourself more" to "God, help me show others that confidence doesn't have to be loud."

- Flip "You should stick with 'fine' when someone asks how you are" to "God, You didn't create me to wear a mask and hide who I am. Help me live in the fullness and joy of being Your daughter."

- Flip "You should tone it down a bit so other women aren't intimidated" to "God, thank You for making me a bold ambassador for You."

Reflection / Book Club

Maybe you've heard a shout from the world that you should speak up more—or less. Maybe you're struggling to discover the voice God has given you and learn how to use it with confidence. Rest today, knowing that the person God created you to be is wonderful. You aren't too much, and you're not lacking. There is someone in your life who needs to hear the words you have to say—words that are full of truth, love, and encouragement. There is someone God is asking you to influence as you share about the hope and peace you have in Jesus in a way that only you can. Stay alert, aware of the power of your words and the worlds you create when you use them, as you choose to influence more by possibly saying less.

1. Reflect on a time when you didn't speak up although you wanted to—or a time you felt you were speaking too much.

2. Spend some time in prayer, asking God to help you align your plans with His will. Silence what the world is shouting and lean into a quiet moment with God.

3. How can you take an intentional step today to swap criticism for confidence as you embrace quality words instead of a large quantity of them?

4. Think about a time when someone's words made an impact on your life. What did they say, and what was the result? Were the words negative or positive? Were you encouraged or defeated? How has that affected the way you interact with others?

> *God, thank You for showing us all the ways our words matter. We'll never create an entire universe through our words, but help us align our words with Your will so that others might experience a world where You bring hope, healing, and forgiveness. Help us replace our critical thoughts and experiences with confidence as we give You all the honor and glory for what You do in and through us—no matter the quantity of our words. In Jesus' name, amen.*

7

I Should Apologize Less

My great-grandfather used to take his cup of coffee, pour a little on a saucer, and drink it from the dish. My husband's grandmother used to put ice in her milk—but she would wash the ice cubes first. We have family members on both sides who were just purely, unapologetically, themselves—strange little quirks and all. I'm sure if either of them saw us walking around, talking to ourselves with phones in front of our faces as we attempted to capture every moment, share on our social media stories, and video chat with friends, they would think we were pretty…unique…as well.

As we work through this section on quieting the shouts of should about our identity, I want to pause and encourage you. When we start to identify the lies we believe, we can make room for the truth to shine brightly. All this heart work is to help us connect deeply with God so we can be more like Him and embrace the beautiful, quirky, not-meant-to-be-like-everyone-else version of ourselves that He has created us to be. And in a chapter on apologizing less, I'm not sorry about it.

My daughter has developed what she likely thinks is a foolproof way to avoid getting in trouble. At the first sign of disapproval or questioning, she begins shooting off rapid-fire *sorrys*. When the first "I'm sorry" is dismissed in favor of a continued conversation about what actually happened or a potential teaching moment so she learns not to do something again, she will—through tears of questionable authenticity—put "I'm sorry" on repeat. The problem (in addition to how often she interrupts and the fact that she can't possibly hear what we're saying as she talks over us) is that the apology loses its meaning. I would rather have a meaningful conversation where she explains what happened, what she was thinking, and what she would do differently next time than hear an empty apology.

And then I hear myself throughout the day, apologizing for speaking up, not being ready, or asking for something I need. Those *sorry* statements are easy and feel socially appropriate—I don't want to appear needy or bossy or inconvenience someone. But what I'm really saying is that I'm unsure of my own thoughts and opinions, uncomfortable in my own skin, and lacking confidence in areas where I actually have expertise.

In 2010 a team from the University of Waterloo conducted several studies to determine why women apologize so often. Their conclusion? "Men apologize less frequently than women because they have a higher threshold for what constitutes offensive behavior."[1] When asked to imagine a scenario where their actions—not harmful, but possibly irresponsible or inconsiderate—would cause a friend to do poorly on something (a school project, test, interview), women rated their role as more highly offensive than the men did and thus required an apology.

As creatures who were created to be in relationships, learning how—and when—to offer a genuine apology is necessary. But it's also important to swap empty words for empathy so we can live in relationship with one another and move through life with freedom, joy, and confidence. If we're committed to choosing quality words instead of focusing on quantity, as we discussed in the previous chapter, it's also important that we give our friends, family, and coworkers our best. That requires saying what we mean and meaning what we say. Writer Nicolette Amarillas offers a few suggestions we can consider:

1. *Instead of apologizing, offer a solution.* Swap "I'm so sorry I forgot the attachment" for "You are correct—I'll send that information right now."

2. *Try trading remorse for gratitude.* Swap "I'm sorry I'm late" for "Thank you for waiting."

3. *Conclude with a real, authentic apology.* Take time to determine if an apology is truly required, and offer one if it is.[2]

Whether we find ourselves using *sorry* as a way to get out of trouble without putting in the hard work of learning from our mistakes, or it's a habit we've picked up from a world that shouts that we should be overly considerate instead of confident, learning to find the right time—and right way—to apologize is essential to healthy relationships with others. There is actually an apology equation that can help: time plus empathy equals an effective (and well-received) apology. Why? Apologizing too quickly, without showing the other person that you've thought through your actions, can look insincere. Apologize without empathy, and the other person will know that you want to make yourself feel better instead of showing that you can put your pride to the side and care about someone else.[3]

We're not trying to remove apologies from our lives completely. We all sin. We all mess up, hurt people, make mistakes, and need to ask others for forgiveness—and we can love others well and honor God when we apologize appropriately, with humility, grace, and under the right circumstances. Words matter, and we want ours to make a difference.

Without paying much attention, all of us develop verbal habits. (Some of us are still struggling to remove the excessive use of the word *like* from our vocabulary, thanks to the '90s.) Psychologist and life coach Judith Tutin has identified four types of apologies. As you read about them in the list below, reflect on how often you use each type.

- *Reflexive:* You're worried that someone is upset with something you've done, so you apologize to quickly fix things— like when my daughter uses "sorry" to avoid consequences.

- *Assertive:* Again, you're not really sorry, but you're hoping that saying the word will soften a potentially unpopular comment to get what you want—like when you don't really want to go out with friends and use "I'm sorry" to back out of a commitment.

- *Blame-reversing:* This one is the epitome of a passive-aggressive apology, using "sorry" to pass blame on to someone else while you try to look like the good guy—"I'm sorry you're taking this so personally…"

- *Genuine:* This is a true apology, using "sorry" in a way

that mends relationships and typically look like: I'm sorry (I confess what I did wrong and acknowledge how it impacted you, followed by an affirmation about why it was the wrong thing to do and an honest attempt to discover how you would like me to fix the situation). [4]

False, reactive apologies chip away at the power of an authentic, reparation-seeking, empowering, forgiveness-focused apology. We can trade out the instant gratification, control, and conflict avoidance of a quick *sorry* for a humble admission of wrongdoing. We can seek forgiveness—which ultimately gives the other person control.

I can't tell you to stop apologizing. That's not biblical, and it removes an important tool God has given us to use as we love others well with humility and grace. But what you and I can work toward are opportunities to use our words with intention. We can quiet the shout of should when we model our behavior after the beautiful example God has given us through Jesus.

> Words matter, and we want
> ours to make a difference.

And what does the Bible have to say about all this? About a perfectly crafted apology, not much. It appears that God isn't as interested in the exact words we say, but about what happens as a result—reconciliation, forgiveness, and love.

- "When you pray, make sure you forgive the faults of others so that your Father in heaven will also forgive you. But if you withhold forgiveness from others, your Father with-holds forgiveness from you" (Matthew 6:14-15 TPT).

- "Whenever you stand praying, if you have anything against anyone, forgive him, so that your Father in heaven will also forgive you your wrongdoing" (Mark 11:25).

- "If we confess our sins, he is faithful and righteous to for-give us our sins and to cleanse us from all unrighteousness" (1 John 1:9).

When we quiet the shout of should that tells us we apologize too much or we should say "sorry" more, we can swap fake, empty words for empowering words that lead to forgiveness and freedom. Not just for others, but for ourselves as we model what God has done for us. Our faith requires action as we do our part to love others well, believe that what God says is true, and give—and receive—forgiveness.

We aren't supposed to stop apologizing. But what we can do is make sure we're aware of the empty words we say and save our *sorry* for moments when we truly need to ask for forgiveness. When we do that—when we learn to apologize in a way that shows empa-thy for another person and remorse for our own actions—we can empower one another to embrace life as fully forgiven, wanted, wor-thy, and called women. We can look another woman in the eye and show that we see value in her, encourage her to keep running hard after Jesus, and demonstrate to the world around us that we can be strong, capable, mountain-moving women who are humble enough to admit when we're wrong—and smart enough to know when to use our words wisely.

Digging Deeper

> Be kind and compassionate to one another, forgiving
> one another, just as God also forgave you in Christ.
>
> EPHESIANS 4:32

I wonder if Paul, the author of Ephesians, had a greater appreciation for the power of forgiveness than some of the other apostles and early followers of Jesus. If we're looking for a list of unlikely characters to spread the gospel around the world, Paul's name would be at the top.

When we first meet Paul in the book of Acts, he is named Saul and is present at the stoning of Stephen (Acts 7:58), who had just stood before the Sanhedrin and given a detailed account of all that God had done for His people. The religious leaders didn't react well to Stephen's pointed message that they, like their ancestors, were ignoring the Holy Spirit, and they had Stephen dragged out of the city to be put to death. Saul must have been there to hear Stephen forgive them before he died (verse 60).

It would be a much nicer story to say that Saul was touched by Stephen's love for God and decided to change his ways then and there. But as we continue to read in Acts (we will get back to Ephesians, I promise), here's what we read about Saul who is not yet Paul:

- "Saul, however, was ravaging the church" (8:3).

- "Now Saul was still breathing threats and murder against the disciples of the Lord" (9:1).

No, Saul would need an even more dramatic encounter with God before he changed his ways. And that encounter came as Saul was traveling to Damascus. While he was on the road, on his way to deliver a letter that would give him the authority to imprison Christians, a light from heaven appeared. Saul fell to the ground and heard the voice of Jesus asking, "Saul, Saul, why are you persecuting me?" (9:4). The men who were with Saul could hear the conversation but could see no one—and when Saul stood up, he discovered that he was blind. For three days he stayed in Damascus, unable to see and unwilling to eat or drink.

Enter Ananias. He knew that Saul had received permission to arrest any followers of Jesus whom he encountered, and yet he was asked by God to find Saul, lay hands on him, and restore his vision. It's no wonder Ananias was hesitant. Go and heal the guy who was out to kill everyone who loved and followed Jesus?

God's response is a beautiful reminder that He can see the big picture beyond our current circumstances, and our obedience may just be the turning point in the life of someone who has yet to have a relationship with Jesus. "Go," said the Lord, "for this man is my chosen instrument to take my name to Gentiles, kings, and Israelites. I will show him how much he must suffer for my name" (Acts 9:15-16).

So Ananias found Saul and laid his hands on him. Saul's sight was restored, and he was filled with the Holy Spirit, baptized, and immediately "began proclaiming Jesus in the synagogues" in Damascus (verse 20). Before long the tables were turned and the Jews were out to kill Saul, so he escaped the city, arrived in Jerusalem, and tried to join the disciples (who, understandably, were hesitant to believe he had changed and wasn't just there to kill them). But Barnabas stood up for him, and Saul began sharing about God throughout the city (verse 28).

Skip ahead to Acts 13, and we read that the Holy Spirit requested that Barnabas and Saul be set apart for missionary work (verse 2). It is in verse 9 where we first read that Saul is now called Paul. God had a plan for a man named Saul who hated Christians—and ultimately that plan led to the writing of almost half of the books of the New Testament. Saul received forgiveness from Stephen when he didn't deserve it, found healing through Ananias when he didn't ask for it, was defended and accepted by the disciples when he wasn't yet known, and was called by God before he made the decision to follow Jesus.

Let's return to the book of Ephesians. Paul has written a letter to the Christians in Ephesus, which was delivered by his messenger Tychicus (Ephesians 6:21-22) because Paul was under house arrest. A little time in jail couldn't stop Paul from his ministry, and his goal with this particular letter was to encourage unity in the church through the power of the Spirit.

> I, the prisoner in the Lord, urge you to live worthy of the calling you have received, with all humility and gentleness, with patience, bearing with one another in love, making every effort to keep the unity of the Spirit through the bond of peace. There is one body and one Spirit—just as you were called to one hope at your calling—one Lord, one faith, one baptism, one God and Father of all, who is above all and through all and in all (4:1-6).

Think about a time when you received advice from someone who had absolutely no experience or expertise in the subject. How did you respond? You probably rolled your eyes, sarcastically thanked them, and ignored absolutely everything they suggested. Now think about a time when someone you respected—someone whom you knew had walked a similar path, experienced similar struggles, and had come out the other side with joy, healing, and hope—offered you guidance. You probably took notes, felt encouraged, and applied their advice to your circumstances.

If someone is going to talk to me about "bearing with one another in love" (4:2), "speaking the truth in love" (verse 15), and "forgiving one another, just as God also forgave you" (verse 32), I want to know that they've been there, done that. I want to know that they understand how hard it is, that the words we say and how we say them truly matter, and that forgiveness is a gift to the giver and receiver. Paul's life was a testimony to the power of forgiveness and the work of the Holy Spirit, and the Christians in Ephesus could trust and believe that he knew what he was talking about. His was guidance they could follow because it was rooted in God's truth.

Everything Paul lays out in Ephesians 4 is rooted in what he previously said in the first three chapters. He started his letter focused on salvation, reminding the believers in Ephesus that it's not something they—or anyone—could achieve through their work or on their own merit. We must spend time dwelling on what God has done for us—how we are saved by grace—before moving on to what we're to do in response.

The way we speak to one another is a reflection of who we believe God is and what He has done for us. Which means our empty words full of fake apologies can never lead to the kind of forgiveness that brings freedom and joy. May the words we use—words of intention, empathy, and love—reflect what God has done for us. Ours is not an empty promise of salvation full of false forgiveness and insignificant change, but a gift freely given that brings freedom and unmistakable life change.

> May the words we use—words of intention, empathy, and love—reflect what God has done for us.

Flip the Script

- Flip "You should wait for the other person to apologize first" to "God, I know You call me to forgive first; help me be an example of Your love to everyone in my life."

- Flip "You should stop apologizing all the time" to "God, I want to be humble and acknowledge my mistakes when it's truly appropriate."

- Flip "You should make sure every apology includes at least four complicated steps in order for it to count" to "God, thank You for showing me what love and forgiveness look like in simple but profound actions that I can share with others."

Reflection / Book Club

Asking God to show us what lies we're believing is a good first step, but it's not the end. Once we know better, we do better, right? It's one thing to identify something in our lives that needs to change, but it's another thing altogether to choose to lay down our old ways of life and embrace something new. A new way of thinking, hosting, loving, speaking, forgiving.

1. Over the next week, pay attention to how often you apologize. Keep a notecard with you or send a quick email

to yourself to track when you say "sorry," what you're apologizing about, and whether or not it's really required in that situation. Ask God to help you put away old habits and empty words so you can work, serve, and love with confidence.

2. Think about a time when you received an apology from someone that felt empty. Why did it feel that way? How did it make you feel about that situation? Now, think about a time when someone offered you a genuine apology and asked for your forgiveness. How did it impact your relationship with that person?

3. Spend some time in God's Word and ask Him to help you find a verse that will help you quiet this shout of should from the world so you can hear Him better.

God, thank You for giving us examples of beautiful, authentic, empowering forgiveness in Your Word. Help us watch what we say, not only so we speak words that encourage and lift up others, but so the words we say reflect Your character. You do not offer us fake hope, but true love. In Jesus' name, amen.

8

I Should Stop Worrying and Be Happier

Nearly all my sleepless nights have started with a question: "What if…?" I could fill in the blank with any number of possibilities, like, "What if we all catch that virus?" or, "What if I'm not cut out to do this?" I'm an equal-opportunity worrier—I worry about past hurts, present struggles, and all sorts of unlikely possibilities for the future. I worry for myself, and also for my husband, daughter, extended family, and friends. If there's a problem, I'll probably stay up all night overthinking it.

In his book *How to Stop Worrying and Start Living*, Dale Carnegie writes, "Our fatigue is often caused not by work, but by worry, frustration, and resentment." It's never the work that keeps me up at night or from doing what God has called me to do, but the parts that I can't control. The *What if?* and *Should I?* and *I wish* thoughts zoom around in my head as I'm trying to sleep, work, or focus on my family. And knowing that I should worry less makes me worry about worrying. I wonder how I'm supposed to be happier and less anxious, and I worry that I'm failing at worrying. It's a terrible cycle.

Here's a new what-if we can explore together: What if we could swap worry for wonder? Instead of feeling anxious about what we can't change or control, could we choose instead to focus on just one wonderful thing God is doing in that circumstance? Is He up to something that reveals His wonder and majesty? Is there some small moment of beauty that we can embrace in wonder, instead of allowing worry to keep us in the dark?

What if we could swap worry for wonder?

On the one hand, worry and anxiety result in tension, poor sleep, irritability, fatigue, problems concentrating, and general unhappiness. On the other hand, worry can help keep us alive as we take precautions to stay healthy, drive more safely, and pay attention to our surroundings.[1] Some of the most common justifications for worry include:

- *If I worry, I'll never have a bad surprise.*
- *It's safer if I worry.*
- *I show I care by worrying.*
- *Worrying motivates me.*
- *Worrying helps me solve problems.*

I'm sure I've used at least one of those reasons to justify my worry. If I don't take the time to overthink a situation, who will? Most suggestions to combat anxiety, like living in the present and facing our fears, are still completely internal and focused on what we can do in our own power. When we turn all our attention inward and attempt to change how we think, feel, or act in our own strength, we will find—at best—temporary solutions that fail to dig out the root of the problem.

My husband is a self-taught lawn care expert who would tell you that the only way to remove what you don't want from your yard is to dig it out by the roots or kill it. Any small piece of that weed or plant that remains in the ground will always come back. Clearing away the ugliness on the surface but failing to address the deeper issue is a temporary fix that will cost you more time and energy in the future.

Whether we're trying to change the way we think, address a sin issue, or deal with our worry, anything other than giving it completely over to Jesus and relying on His help will leave us holding on to the tiny parts we think we can handle. Eventually, those anxieties will grow back, and we'll find ourselves in the same place, with the same struggles, wondering why we can't fix the worry on our own.

If you've ever lain awake at night with your mind racing, you might not be surprised to learn that sleep deprivation plays a big role in how we manage worry and anxiety. One article from Harvard Medical School explores the connection between sleep and mental health. Taking longer to fall asleep, having trouble staying asleep, and not getting enough sleep can add up and take a serious toll on our health. "Sleep disruption...wreaks havoc in the brain, impairing thinking and emotional regulation."[2] The more disrupted our sleep, the more we struggle to process what we're worrying about in a healthy, productive way—which means we sleep less, and the cycle continues. Maybe we should try to go to bed a little earlier.

Before science declared it, God designed it. He created us to require rest, and He designed our world to have day and night, times to be awake and times to sleep. He modeled rest for us at creation, and Jesus exemplified it in His ministry. In Mark 6, before we get to the story of Jesus feeding the 5,000, we see the disciples gathered around Him. They reported back all that they had been doing: preaching, casting out demons, and anointing and healing the sick. Jesus then gave them this invitation: "He said to them, 'Come away by yourselves to a remote place and rest for a while.' For many people were coming and going, and they did not even have time to eat" (Mark 6:31).

God is fully aware that we can push ourselves to our limits, working late and rising early, caring for others more than ourselves. He knew we would need a model, a specific reason to stop and rest, to recharge so we could face each day with grace.

Before science declared it, God designed it.

When we choose to stop and reflect on what God has done in our day, in the relationships He's placed in our lives, in the beauty of a sunset or the laughter of our kids, we can begin to teach our brains to seek wonder instead of worry. And when we take time to be with God, aligning our lives with His will, we can find freedom in letting go of the expectation to be happy and embrace the lasting, fulfilling joy of choosing holiness.

I love to travel, but I hate getting somewhere. In the week leading up to any vacation or work trip, my mind races through to-do lists, packing lists, timelines, and what-ifs. Do I pack everything in a checked bag so I can move quickly through the airport with freedom, or do I take the carry-on so I can make sure none of my luggage will be lost when we land? What will I do if I get stuck at the airport? Who is picking me up, and where am I meeting them? If I pack light, will I regret not having options? If I pack clothing options, will I actually wear them? What if traffic is bad on the way to the airport? We should probably give ourselves a lot of extra time, just in case.

Yes, I am the one in the security line with my shoes off, ID in hand, and laptop already out of my bag even before I get to the metal detectors.

Several years ago, I was getting ready for my first official work trip for a new job. I was packed, had my itinerary, knew how I was getting to the airport…and then it snowed. A lot. Suddenly, all my carefully orchestrated plans were out the window, and I was panicking and scrambling to fix the situation. When the alert came through my email that my flight had been canceled, I read through the instructions to book a new flight, clicked some links, confirmed my new flight, and arranged a new ride to the airport for the next day.

Imagine my surprise when my phone reminded me later that afternoon that my flight was boarding—as I was sitting at home enjoying a cup of coffee. Sure, I had successfully rescheduled my flight—but not for the next day like I'd planned; it was for that *same* day. Now there was no way I could fix the problem on my own. A humbling email to the travel coordinator admitting my mistake resulted in new tickets (for the correct day) but a less-than-stellar impression.

Worry has led me into more mistakes than I'd care to admit as I've scrambled to try to fix something without taking the time to ask for help, step back, or understand all my options. And when flights *do* get canceled or family members *do* fall ill, I feel my anxieties are justified…which only makes me more worried the next time a similar situation arises. Worry tells my brain not to believe what my heart knows. My heart trusts God and has faith that He is fully in control, while my brain finds little ways to hold on to some of that control—just in case.

> Worry tells my brain not to believe what my heart knows.

Worry keeps us in the dark, and we miss the beauty of the journey. We miss the hope, joy, and peace that come from trusting God. We miss the opportunity to develop patience, perseverance, compassion, and empathy that comes when we commit to going through the hard things without preparing for a battle that may never arrive. The opposite of worrying less isn't to be happy all the time, but to seek wonder—God's hand and presence—in all our circumstances. And as we do that, as we intentionally shift our focus away from what *we* can do to what *God* has promised to do, we can spend our time working on the things that matter—the small next steps that help us grow to be more like Christ.

This week keep a small notebook nearby. Whenever you find yourself overwhelmed with worry, write about it, answering these questions:

- *What am I worried about?*

- *What do I wish my worry would fix about this situation?*

- *What "best-case scenario" can I focus on instead?*

Then, at the end of the day, flip through your notebook and turn those "wish" statements into prayers. Imagine that each of those worries is a big, heavy rock. Picture yourself carrying them to the foot of the cross. Every worst-case scenario, fear, uncertainty, anxious thought, and lie goes before Jesus. Each stone has your worry written on it, and when you leave it in the loving, powerful, wise hands of Jesus, imagine the weight of that worry lifting off you. Roll your shoulders down and away from your ears. Relax and breathe. Thank God for taking care of the things you can't change.

Our prayers are powerful, but God's promises are perfect. Trust Him.

Digging Deeper

> Don't worry about anything, but in everything,
> through prayer and petition with
> thanksgiving, present your requests to God. And the
> peace of God, which surpasses all understanding, will
> guard your hearts and minds in Christ Jesus.
>
> PHILIPPIANS 4:6-7

Our quest to swap happiness for holiness is really a journey to become more like Christ, and Paul's letter to the believers in Philippi is like a road map for that journey. Paul gives us basic, down-to-earth advice about working without grumbling, remaining humble, and exalting Christ in all we do.

In the closing chapter of the book, Paul not only instructs the believers not to worry, but he also offers a practical solution to their anxiety:

> Finally brothers and sisters, whatever is true, whatever is honorable, whatever is just, whatever is pure, whatever is lovely, whatever is commendable—if there is any moral excellence and if there is anything praiseworthy—dwell on these things. Do what you have learned and received and heard from me, and seen in me, and the God of peace will be with you (Philippians 4:8-9).

How do we swap worry for wonder? By training our minds to seek what is true, honorable, just, pure, lovely, and commendable. By surrounding ourselves with people who do this well and can serve as examples on days when we need encouragement. And by trusting that God will fill our hearts and minds with peace. He will guard us from the advances of the enemy—an enemy who will try to keep us so distracted through worrying about the things we cannot change, or so disappointed in our pursuit of fleeting happiness, that we will fail to do the quiet, daily, obedient work to become more like Christ.

In the same way that God knew we would need His example of work and rest in Genesis, it's comforting to realize that He has also provided guidance for every other area in which we might struggle. From examples of prayer to stories of forgiveness, instruction on how to be a good friend to a passage that tells us not to worry, God knows exactly what we need. It's not easy to imagine that someone in prison would write a letter about being "content whatever the circumstances" (Philippians 4:11 NIV), but Paul's faith and the story of his life serve as a reminder on our hardest days: True joy and peace don't come from what we do or what happens to us, but from God.

Years ago, when I worked for an online ministry, I remember sitting around a table with some of the women, talking about books we were enjoying. My daughter was still very little at the time, and I was happy to read almost any book on motherhood and parenting that came my way. I was sharing about one I'd recently finished by an author who also had young children, and I remember one of the other women saying, "I don't want to read books by someone who is still in it—I want to hear from someone who survived it."

She made an interesting point. There are times when we need to be encouraged by someone in our same season, or someone who is still in the middle of what we're going through. It helps us feel less alone. But there are also times when what we really need is to hear from someone who has made it through to the other side and can offer not just empathy but wisdom. When I hear someone's story and realize that I could be *there* in a few years? It gives me hope. I trust what they say because they've gone on the journey first. They know the obstacles to avoid, the beautiful moments to look for, and the joy of making it through.

The Philippians knew they could trust Paul. If he, who had been arrested, beaten, and imprisoned on his first visit to their city years before (Acts 16), could find a way to dwell on things that please God, they could too. They knew that Paul spent his time in their prison *rejoicing*, "singing hymns to God" (verse 25), not moaning about his bad luck or worrying about tomorrow.

You and I can spend all our spare time worrying about our circumstances, what might happen, or what the world shouts that we should be doing. But worry doesn't grow God's kingdom. The people God has put in your life won't be drawn to Him because they've watched you worry about something. But they might want to know more about God when they see you face life with unexplainable joy, peace, and wonder.

For myself, I don't want to pass down a legacy of worry to my daughter. I want her to know the freedom that comes from silencing the shouts of should and focusing on the wonder of a God who speaks in a still, quiet voice.

Flip the Script

- Flip "You should worry less" to "God, thank You for giving me a heart that cares for others; help me discern how to worry wisely."

- Flip "You should never worry if you trust God" to "God, help me show my trust in You as I bring every concern and worry to the cross."

- Flip "You should always be happy" to "God, life isn't always easy, but I'm so grateful that You get the glory no matter my circumstances."

Reflection / Book Club

Before we wrap up this chapter, let me say this: If what you are struggling with is more than worry, if it's something bigger and deeper than what a chapter in a book can help with, please find someone to talk to. I wouldn't have been able to share my story with you without counseling, wise doctors, medicine, prayer, and community. Take care of yourself, okay?

Long after you've finished reading this book, and you find yourself worrying about something, you didn't fail at this "quieting the shout of should" stuff. We are going to worry. We're going to be concerned about the safety of our loved ones, make plans to ensure that we'll catch our plane on time, and go over the to-do list one last time to make sure we're not missing anything before that big event at work. What we're trying not to do is allow our worry to take up more space in our lives than it deserves. Here are a few verses to keep nearby over the coming weeks that can help you swap worry for wonder:

- "Come to me, all of you who are weary and burdened, and I will give you rest. Take up my yoke and learn from me, because I am lowly and humble in heart, and you will find rest for your souls. For my yoke is easy and my burden is light" (Matthew 11:28-30).

- "I will both lie down and sleep in peace, for you alone, LORD, make me live in safety" (Psalm 4:8).

- "You will keep the mind that is dependent on you in perfect peace, for it is trusting in you" (Isaiah 26:3).

- "I have told you these things so that in me you may have peace. You will have suffering in this world. Be courageous! I have conquered the world" (John 16:33).

1. Which one of the verses listed above do you connect with most strongly?

2. In the last few weeks, what have you worried about? How did worrying shape your circumstances? How would the results have been different if you had chosen to find wonder, joy, and peace instead—and how could you have swapped

worry for something that pointed you back to God? For example, when your mind wanders to all the ways a loved one could get hurt driving home from school or work, you could choose instead to say a prayer of thanksgiving for all the ways God has protected them thus far.

3. In your journal or with your group, brainstorm practical ways to keep your mind focused on what is true, honorable, just, pure, lovely, commendable, and praiseworthy. What would you include on that list?

> *God, thank You for knowing every struggle we'll face and every shout the world will hurl at us, and thank You for giving us Your Word to guide us through. Help us seek wonder instead of worry so we can influence others for Your kingdom through our unexplainable joy and peace as we grow to be more like Christ—not happier, but holy. As it says in Philippians 4:19-20, supply all our needs according to Your riches in glory in Christ Jesus, and to You be the glory forever and ever. In Jesus' name, amen.*

Quiet Time

Remember the Words of the Lord

In every way I've shown you that it is necessary to help the weak
by laboring like this and to remember the words of the Lord
Jesus, because he said, "It is more blessed to give than to receive."

ACTS 20:35

Read Acts 20:32-35

This past summer, a group of ragtag kids from various small towns in our area came together for Vacation Bible School and, over the course of four days, raised more than $400 to help other students purchase school supplies. It is amazing what kids and their parents will do when a church pits girls against boys in a friendly competition to see who can bring in more money each night. It's even more incredible to watch how deep the parents' pockets suddenly are when they want their child to be on the winning team—because we all know those six-year-olds aren't out working hard for that $20 bill they just donated.

Somehow, regardless of the competition, I think these kids got it. My own daughter was in the mix—and I know that her mind is generally more "me" focused than service oriented. But her heart also hurts when she knows there are kids who don't have food when they go home or families who love them. She has raised money at lemonade stands to help provide food for children in other countries, but she is also the one who pouted when she didn't get the overpriced slushy at the amusement park.

My heart can be like that too. I have dreams of one day being able to offer scholarships and mentoring for other writers, but I also want that cute new jacket. Today's scripture is one we can cling to when our good intentions for service are being undermined by our selfishness.

In the previous verses, Paul begins to wrap up his speech to the early church by reminding them that he has worked hard to earn the financial provisions he and his team need. He encourages the church to continue to work hard and to give generously to those who aren't able to support themselves.

"It is more blessed to give than to receive" (Acts 20:35) is a great quote to hang in your home but a hard one to live out on a daily basis. Giving feels like a sacrifice. Receiving feels like a gift. Giving focuses on the needs of someone else. Receiving focuses the attention on what we want.

There will be seasons for both. But when I compare the joy on my daughter's face after she's helped other students to the look of fleeting gratitude when she picks out her own school supplies at the store, I see the difference. We can make a difference.

Quiet Quest

When was the last time you gave generously out of your available resources—time, money, expertise—without expecting anything in return? How can a life of intentional generosity quiet the shouts of should that fill our homes with things and keep us distracted from Jesus?

Use it to Serve

*Just as each one has received a gift, use it to serve
others, as good stewards of the varied grace of God.*

1 PETER 4:10

Read 1 Peter 4:10-11

My husband won a certificate at a local Italian restaurant that says he is "Matt the Great." It was presented with much fanfare and laughter at the end of a meal with family. The reason for his award? He finished his lasagna.

To be fair, it was a rather large, apparently difficult-to-finish portion of pasta. No other item on the menu came with the promise of a reward, but my husband is not one to back away from a challenge. (Consider the next day, when he did 50 push-ups to earn a free shirt.) The best part? As the manager was filling out his certificate, Matt moved on to dessert! Apparently, this isn't normal behavior for most people who eat that much lasagna, because the manager was equally impressed and concerned.

While remarkable, this was definitely not the kind of gift Peter had in mind in today's reading. We have all been given gifts to use to serve others and give glory to God. When we work within those gifts, when we focus on the talents we have instead of the skills we think we should have been given, we serve with energy and enthusiasm. It's not a drain on our resources when we work within our gifting—somehow, we find room to accomplish more when others wonder how we do it. We find joy in writing, speaking, teaching, hosting, volunteering, managing, serving, creating, or building when we work from the strength God provides. When we love others well through the gifts God has given us, there is always room for just a little more.

Quiet Quest

If you haven't done it recently, this is a good time to set that timer on your phone and spend some quality quiet time with the Lord. Consider increasing your time by a few minutes today and move your phone across the room. Go to God in prayer, asking Him to help you make room for more and to reveal where the shoulds have distracted you from His plan for your life. Where have you abandoned your gifts because they didn't feel impressive enough, the amount you had to give felt lacking, or because you tried to use them and failed? What is one small way you can step back into the role God has created for you?

Well Seasoned

Let your speech always be gracious,
seasoned with salt.

COLOSSIANS 4:6

Read Colossians 4:6

The right words at the right time can be life giving. Confusing words (like the time someone cornered me at a conference to say God had given her a message for me that included a story about a bunny) can be distracting. Harsh words can be defeating and discouraging. Our words and the ways we use them are important and can mean the difference between piling more shoulds on someone or helping them walk in the freedom for which God designed them.

I'm currently working with an organization called Love God Greatly. They write Bible studies for women and make them available for free, and they work with a team of translators to make sure that women around the world have access to the studies in their own language. My role is entirely behind the scenes, but I've heard the stories of God moving in mighty ways through small groups of women who are committed to sharing the gospel.

Their work and words are seasoned with salt—the kind that is life giving and adds brightness and flavor to each interaction. The studies and conversations aren't bland or boring—they are sprinkled with personal testimonies and shared experiences, served over a solid layer of God's Word. Scripture is more than enough on its own, but when we share it with others through gracious words and a dash of God's work in our lives, we can invite them into the beauty of God's living, active, never-boring Word.

Quiet Quest

Think for a few minutes about someone in your life who has shown you what it looks like to use gracious words that are seasoned with salt. Write down what they said, how they said it, and how it pointed you to Jesus. Consider writing them a letter or sending them an email to let them know how much those words meant—or write down a few ways you can share that legacy through your own words.

Be Transformed

Be transformed by the renewing of your mind.

ROMANS 12:2

Read Romans 12:2

There is a church camp in the woods about 30 minutes from our house. When I was younger and able to recover more quickly from sleep deprivation, I volunteered with friends to serve for several years as a camp counselor for eighth grade girls. Now that it takes me a week to recover from one night of bad sleep, Madi and I go to that same camp for a mother-daughter overnight trip.

Part of the camp experience is vespers at a place called Brenneman Chapel. We follow a path, crossing under a sign declaring, "Silence." No one speaks on the trail to the outdoor chapel—a clearing in the woods where someone thoughtfully crafted wooden benches and a small stone stage. The request for quiet prepares our hearts for worship and gives our ears the opportunity to hear what is happening around us. Birds, bugs, water, wind—all the little sounds that are usually hidden under our own voices.

It's a moment to renew our minds as we give our senses a break from the noise. In the quiet we can hear our own thoughts, focus on our prayers, worship with our whole hearts and no distractions. The world shouts at us to conform, but what we really need is to be transformed. To make a shift that swaps our scattered thoughts for a singular focus: Jesus. In the silence we can stop trying to do it all and simply be with the One who created it all, and out of that overflow—as we walk out of that space—we can work and love and serve with peace and purpose.

Quiet Quest

Is there a place in your life that could benefit from a little *silence* sign? A reminder as you enter your office, car, or favorite reading nook that, because Jesus lives in us, even those spaces can be holy ground? Whether you write the word on a sticky note or go to one of those "make your own sign" workshops, add a visual reminder somewhere special and practice settling your heart and quieting your mind each time you enter that space.

Good and Perfect Gifts

*Every good and perfect gift is from above, coming down from
the Father of lights, who does not change like shifting shadows.*

JAMES 1:17

Read James 1:2-17

Today's final verse, read on its own, always reminds me of Christmas. Good and perfect gifts! Who doesn't love those? In fact, many of us pride ourselves on being experts in finding good and perfect gifts for everyone on our list. The spouse who buys everything he wants when he needs it? The friend at work who likes nothing and has everything? The secret gift swap at your child's school that has high expectations for something under five dollars? We've got this. This is why we shop the clearance section at Target all year, right?

But what James is really talking about in this chapter is the power of perseverance through trials, along with a stern reminder that God is not the one tempting us. The verses that precede today's featured scripture point out that choosing to follow our own desires leads to sin. When the enemy tempts us away from God's will, from the narrow path He has created for us, and we grasp for all that the world offers—the shiny, sparkly, noisy, distracting, self-centered—the only thing we get at the end is separation from God.

Do not be deceived. That temptation does not come from God. He doesn't offer us life one moment and tempt us into sin the next. That's not His character. If we stick with Him, if we endure and stay humble, He has good gifts for us. As James reminds us, "The gifts are rivers of light cascading down from the Father of Light. There is nothing deceitful in God, nothing two-faced, nothing fickle. He brought us to life using the true Word, showing us off as the crown of all his creatures" (James 1:17-18 MSG).

And these are gifts we'll never find on the clearance shelf.

Quiet Quest

Think about a time when chasing your own desires only drew you further away from God. What were the small, seemingly insignificant decisions you made along the way that caused you to go after what you thought you deserved? How did those choices ultimately impact your faith, your friendships, your family? If you're in that season now, what is one thing you can do to turn back to God?

Part 3

Time and
Talents

9

I Should Work Less and Serve More

We all work. Each of us holds a different title, experience, set of talents and passions, but we all perform work every day. Whether that happens in an office, a grocery store, on a college campus, in our homes, or as we faithfully and quietly show up to do tasks behind the scenes that no one sees—we work. And somewhere along the way, we've all wondered if we're doing the right work, if we're working too much, and if there is something better we should be doing.

Let's make sure we're on the same page with a few things before we dive into this topic. First, no matter how hard it is to drag ourselves to the office on Monday morning, work isn't a result of sin entering the world. Genesis records God's beautiful example of working hard and resting well during the act of creation. We also see that He assigned work to Adam: "The LORD God took the man and placed him in the garden of Eden to work it and watch over it" (Genesis 2:15). When

Adam and Eve chose to ignore God's command and sin entered the world, they were separated from Him. Everything that was provided for them in Eden would now require hard, painful labor to produce. Work is not the enemy—Satan is.

Second, we all have work to do that builds God's kingdom. Yes, we also have work to do that provides for our basic necessities, like food, clothing, and shelter. But we're here for much more than that. We're not here to build our own kingdoms, but to share the gospel with those who need to know the hope of Jesus. Shortly after Jesus was resurrected, He appeared to 11 of the disciples on a mountain in Galilee. While there He assigned them—and each of us, by extension—specific work to do: "Go, therefore, and make disciples of all nations, baptizing them in the name of the Father and of the Son and of the Holy Spirit, teaching them to observe everything I have commanded you. And remember, I am with you always, to the end of the age" (Matthew 28:19-20). God doesn't wrap any other requirements around that commission. We can use our unique talents, location, and personality as we do the work He has called us to do.

At the same time, it's easy to look around and feel torn in several directions. Maybe, like me, you love to work but feel caught between your desire to enjoy the life God has given you and the pull to work harder, longer hours to keep up with all your goals—especially when you see what other women are doing in similar fields. Research has shown that the United States is "the most overworked developed nation in the world." We pride ourselves on hard work, celebrate promotions and advancement, and have a mental list of what we need to own or achieve to be considered successful. Yet we're overworked and overwhelmed. If you live in the United States, you can understand this constant tension. We're not meant to work without rest, but we live in a culture that rewards striving.

What are we afraid of? If we slow down and take time off, will our productivity really suffer? If we step back for a season or rest for a moment, will we be replaced or overlooked?

Andoni Aduriz is the chef and owner of Mugaritz, a restaurant located near San Sebastián, Spain. Mugaritz is considered one of the ten best restaurants in the world. You would assume that a highly recognized, world-famous, award-winning restaurant would require nonstop work with little time off. But Aduriz closes his restaurant for four months every year. He and his team use the time to do research and development so they can create their next menu, testing nearly 500 recipes to discover the 70 that will make it onto the menu.[1]

More work doesn't necessarily equal more productivity. And less work doesn't necessarily produce more rest. In order to quiet the shouts of should that tell us that our work needs to look a certain way, or that we can't collaborate without fear of competition, or that we should ignore our talents and serve in just one specific way, we need to be willing to ignore the script and simply say "yes." A "yes" to wherever God is leading us and however He is using us.

When we're overwhelmed with all we need to do, should do, have to do—all comparisons based on someone else's life—we can find ourselves with decision paralysis. It happens to me, every year, around the holidays. In addition to the personal list of shopping, hosting, decorating, and finding memorable activities to do with my family, I also work in ministry. Which means October through January can be summed up as the "most frantic time of the year." There are invitations to print, special graphics to request, a minimum of eight services before Christmas Eve, staff parties and community outreach events to attend, devotions to publish, decorating committees to join, year-end planning to handle, and the typical day-to-day list of items to complete. As a department of one. I'll give you a minute to insert your own busy list here, and then maybe you can relate to what happens next.

Instead of focusing on just one thing that needs to get done, we do nothing. Or we flit around like little hummingbirds, zipping to this project and that task and starting something new every few minutes but never actually finishing anything. If we do happen to miraculously complete one of the projects we're working on, we never stop long enough to celebrate it or acknowledge the work we've done—we just rush off to the next thing because we feel like we need to keep proving our worth through our work.

Is it any surprise that studies show women suffer high rates of burnout? The World Health Organization now recognizes burnout as a syndrome connected to chronic stress at work.[2] It can look like a lack of motivation, feelings of helplessness and depression, and physical symptoms like chronic headaches or sickness, because stress suppresses the immune system. We're in a cultural season where hustle (the kind that goes 24-7) is rewarded and the workday looks more like the Industrial Revolution era when laws had to be created to protect people (including children) from working 16-hour days. Our ability to work from anywhere, at any time, means we often feel like we're on call without the ability to unplug.

So how do we swap paralysis for progress? Not by working less, which would seem like the obvious answer. Instead, we do it by choosing intentional rest that recharges us for the work God has called us to do, putting boundaries on our time, and finding ways to give back.

Researchers are discovering that volunteering and serving have mental and physical benefits that might just be what we need. As Stephanie Watson puts it, "People who donate their time feel more socially connected, thus warding off loneliness and depression. But...a growing body of evidence suggests that people who give their time to others might also be rewarded with better *physical* health—including lower blood pressure and a longer lifespan."[3]

I wish I could give you a simple formula that says, "Working this many hours plus serving others this many hours equals health, happiness, and motivation." I would easily schedule my entire life around that equation if I could, putting hard and fast boundaries around anything that didn't fit within those limits. But life just doesn't work that way, and our changing seasons would shift our availability and ability. Here's what we can trust: God has created good work for us to do (Ephesians 2:10); He has modeled rest for us (Genesis 2:3); we are to use our talents to serve others (1 Peter 4:10). When we feel the weight of the world pressing down on us, and we don't feel like we can possibly do one more thing, God invites us to give Him our heavy burdens (Matthew 11:28-30). You can do all that is before you—not because you have the talent, time, or tenacity, but because God is there with you every step of the way.

Each bar that I take out of the box to display is more beautiful than the last. Swirls of color perfectly match the scents that come wafting my way, tops sprinkled with just the right amount of glitter. Tiny stamps pressed into the bar, simple packaging, thoughtful artistry. Knowing the care that has gone into each bar makes selling these handmade soaps for my mom's company easy.

We spend months preparing for craft shows that last a few hours, knowing we'll have a customer who prefers the mass-produced, no-longer-actually-soap versions they can buy at a dollar store. Which is, somehow, worse than watching someone's child "smell" the soap by shoving the bar up their nose—or taking a small bite out of the corner.

But we also know we'll meet people who appreciate the work it takes to combine ingredients in such a specific way to achieve what we're offering. They'll listen appreciatively as we answer their questions about the process, the weeks it takes to produce a bar of soap that we're proud to present. They'll ask smart questions, taking their time to find exactly what they want, and we'll see them over and over again throughout the season. If you're picturing a middle-aged woman shopping, you're not wrong—but you're also missing the teenager who has the heart of an artist, the male college student who is kind and funny, the young woman who would one day like to do exactly what we're doing. You're forgetting about the elementary school student who freely offers compliments about everything she loves and spends her own money to buy something special, just for her.

I've learned more about work, rest, and serving the community as I've helped at Middle Spring Soap Company than anywhere else. I've learned that work done well is worth the time it takes to get it right, and that rushing the process and trying to multitask usually means more work in the end, fixing mistakes. On the days when we're up before the sun to set up for a show that may or may not earn back the money we paid to be there, we've learned to find value in serving people well. We make friends with our vendor neighbors and support their businesses; we smile and show interest in the people who have kindly stopped to shop; and we always forget to count calories on craft show days. And when my mom finds an organization who could serve others well with what she makes, she generously donates.

Work done well is worth the time it takes to get it right.

With my marketing background I could honestly sell anything my mom makes. I mean, I sold checking accounts to people during the 2008 financial crisis. But to know that my mom refuses to sell anything that isn't high quality makes my job easy. I've watched her research and develop products for months before finally agreeing to sell them. I've seen her turn down large orders when someone asks her to rush the process, as she knows what she would deliver wouldn't be a great reflection of what she usually makes.

I have a tendency to want to rush the process. I want to get to the end result, to finish what I'm working on, wrap it up beautifully, and push it out the door so I can move on to something else. I like to say "yes" to invitations that feel like the next big thing without considering whether or not it's a right *yes* for right now. I skip around from project to project and wonder why I'm frustrated at the end when I have to go back and fix mistakes. And in all my rushing, producing, working, and creating I forget to see the people in front of me.

The world shouts that we should do whatever it takes to make the most, do the best, and be all things to all people—but not to work too much or share too freely. However, what I'm learning, slowly, is that we can find joy in the work that we do when we serve others with the gifts God has given us and discover progress in the process.

Digging Deeper

> Noah did everything that the LORD commanded him.
>
> GENESIS 7:5

Everything I know about Bible stories for kids I learned from VeggieTales. Well, maybe not everything—but I didn't grow up going to Sunday school, so I have no emotional attachment to or fond memories of flannelgraphs, puppet shows, or whatever other culturally relevant format teachers once used to tell these stories to the five-and-under crowd. (An interesting but not particularly relevant side note: I once met Phil Vischer, the creator of VeggieTales, at a conference for bloggers. He's a lovely man, and it's incredibly odd to hear the voice of a talking tomato come out of the mouth of a grown adult.)

The actual story of Noah, the one we're going to dig into today, is found in Genesis 6–9 and doesn't include any talking vegetables. It's the story of a man who found favor with God and chose to say "yes" to God instead of following the pull of the world into sin. And it's a reminder to us that the work God has given us, the way we serve and love and obey, will make us stand out from the culture around us.

As we read Genesis 6, we see that God was grieved over the constant evil of humanity (verses 5-6). What He had created and called good was now completely corrupt. As one commentary puts it, "God's grief as described here is a mixture of rage and bitter anguish. His regret reflects the idea of breathing or sighing deeply. Out of that regret comes a destructive plan. God's judgment will involve an almost complete erasure of man and all accompanying creatures from existence. God's pain over sin prompts Him to blot out the wicked."[4]

But there was one family chosen to survive. In verse 9 we learn why God chose Noah: "Noah was a righteous man, blameless among his contemporaries; Noah walked with God." Instead of conforming to the world, Noah chose God. And God chose Noah.

As God laid out His plan to Noah, He made two promises: The world and everything in it would be destroyed by floodwaters, but God would protect Noah, his family, and two of every kind of animal on the ark Noah was to build.

Four times in these chapters we read of Noah's complete obedience to God (6:22; 7:5,9,16). Surrounded by evil, Noah chose to say "yes" to the work God gave Him—unprecedented instruction to build a boat that was as long as one and a half football fields and more than four stories tall in modern terms.[5] Instead of listening to the shouts of the world around him, Noah focused on what God told him.

Tremper Longman points out how the record of the flood is "structured by a careful counting of the days," just like the account of creation in Genesis 1. The *Layman's Old Testament Bible Commentary* lists this counting found in Genesis:

- *7 days of waiting for the waters to come (7:4,10)*

- *40 days of water rising (7:12,17)*

- *150 days of waters prevailing (7:24; 8:3)*

- *40 days of water receding (8:6)*

- *7 days of waiting for the waters to recede (8:10)*

- *7 more days of waiting for the waters to recede completely (8:12)*[6]

After endless months in the ark, Noah, his family, and all the creatures were invited by God to come out onto the now-dry land. Noah immediately built an altar to honor God with a sacrifice, and God made a promise to never again destroy every living thing (8:21). In a throwback to God's blessing to Adam, Noah was commissioned to "be fruitful and multiply and fill the earth" (9:1). God made an eternal covenant with Noah and all who would come after him to never again flood the earth, using a rainbow as a way to remember His promise (9:12-17).

God may have been grieved by the sins of humanity, but it did not change His character. He is a God of second chances who desires a relationship with us. He found the one man on earth who quieted the shouts of should (that likely told him he was crazy to build a giant boat on land), abided closely enough with God to hear His commands, and said "yes" without knowing how it all would end.

The work God has for us, the way He invites us to build His kingdom through our service to others, can be scary. But if He has you outside your comfort zone, trust Him. He knows what will happen on the other side, how it will all turn out when you follow in obedience. Those around you may not understand why you work, rest, serve, and love people the way that you do. You might feel the pull toward fitting into a culture that feels easy and accepted. It may be harder to choose grace when you would rather grumble or forgiveness when you would rather fight to earn the place you know you deserve. But our everyday, ordinary acts of obedience will help us say "yes" in the small moments so that, like Noah, we're prepared to honor God with our complete obedience when He presents us with bigger opportunities.

The story of Noah in Genesis doesn't tell us what his family thought of this project or what his neighbors said to him as they watched him build the ark. We don't know how long it took him, or where he had to go to find the supplies he needed. Maybe you've found yourself in a place that feels similarly lonely as you've worked to listen to God's quiet voice over the shouts of the world. You feel set apart—not in a way that makes you feel special, but like an outsider. You're committed to doing the work God has assigned you, but the people around you don't understand, can't see the value, don't grasp the significance.

Keep going. Your obedience today could be the thing that introduces a new generation to the love of God. It's worth it.

Flip the Script

- Flip "You should only want to use your gifts to serve, not work" to "God, every good and perfect gift is from You, and I'm so grateful that I can support my family by using my talents."

- Flip "You should have your career figured out by now" to "God, as stages of my life change, so do my passions. Help me always keep You as the center of everything I'm able to do."

- Flip "You should work more to be more productive" to "God, thank You for creating us to thrive in a balance of work and rest."

Reflection / Book Club

As you reflect on the work you do and the ways you serve, rest in the knowledge that God has created you for a life that is both-and, not either-or. You can work *and* rest, take care of yourself *and* serve others, have boundaries *and* make progress on the goals and dreams God has given you. It is not by your constant work and hectic schedule that you will stand out from the crowd, but by embracing who God made you to be while being a good steward of the time, talents, place, and people you've been given.

If you feel like you're being pushed outside your comfort zone, good! We don't follow God because it's easy. We don't share our faith because it's comfortable. We don't choose the narrow road because it's prettier. But we will never regret a life of obedience as we build God's kingdom instead of our own.

1. Where have you felt stuck in your work? What would it take to begin making progress?

2. How is Noah's obedience encouraging to you as you seek to quiet the shout of should?

3. What lies have you believed lately about the value of your work and the impact of your service? What are the excuses or fears that keep you from fully obeying God in these areas?

4. What is one practical thing you can do this week to work, rest, or serve well? If there is one area that is harder for you to incorporate into your routine, take some time and ask God to reveal why.

God, thank You for being a God of second chances who keeps His promises. As we work, rest, and serve, may we honor You in all we do. Help us embrace feeling uncomfortable and out of place in this world as we become more like Christ. This world is not our final home, but while we're here, let us abide closely with You, hear Your voice, and obey Your Word. In Jesus' name, amen.

10

I Should Have Achieved That Dream by Now

My husband and I had a meeting with our financial adviser the other week to talk about our retirement goals. I mean, if anyone asked me how old I am, it would actually take me some time to remember that I am *not* 28 anymore, so it's hard to realize that these are legitimate conversations that have actual impact in the not-as-far-away-as-I'd-like future. The adviser asked us to think about three financial dreams we have, things we would like to be able to do in the next few years or something we're working toward in retirement. The idea was that we would choose goals to which we could assign dollar amounts so that he could help us get there.

My husband, who probably should have just been a financial adviser anyway, loved it. He had the perfect goals and already knew how much we would need to be able to achieve them. Me? I wasn't so sure.

It's not that I don't have ideas—I usually have too many. But I found myself unable to dream big about the future when my old dreams hadn't come true yet. How do we dream forward when we're afraid that the best has already passed us? And how are we supposed to put dollar signs on something like "help young artists and other writers pursue their dreams"? What is that? A ministry? A scholarship? A class?

Instead of being able to focus on the future, I was trapped in the past as I thought about all the other ideas and goals that never came to fruition, the places I thought I should be by now, the women I know who used to be my peers and who are now known worldwide and do things for God beyond anything I've ever let myself consider. Shouldn't I be "there" by now?

When we compare our lives to someone else's, we lose the ability to dream. We're so caught up in what everyone else is doing that we forget that God has something fantastic planned just for us. Instead of looking excitedly toward the future, we feel weighed down by the pressure of goals unmet, dreams not yet realized, and time speeding past faster than we'd like to admit.

As we dig into quieting the shouts that tell us we should be "there" by now, we're going to explore ways to swap comparison for contentment and discouragement for dreaming. I want us to finish this chapter so filled with holy anticipation about what God can do in and through us that we can't wait to write down all our new dreams. My prayer is that our eyes would be open to the new possibilities and opportunities He puts before us, that we would be blind to comparison and feeling like we're not doing enough and instead find joy in pursuing goals that are so perfectly in line with God's will that we face them without fear of failure. I want us to be women who dream audaciously—not because we're going to become famous for it, but because we can't wait to see how it will make God famous.

I want us to believe that the best is yet to come because I need to believe it too. It's far easier for me to look back at my life and the things I've accomplished and feel like the best has already happened. I've achieved incredible success, met amazing people, traveled the country, had a wonderful family, and checked the only big dream I had off my list when my first book was published. In my race to get to all these places, I'm left feeling stuck and wondering if it's all downhill from here. In my mind, life has been one large bell curve, and I was in a race against myself—and others—to get to the top first. Instead of enjoying a slow climb, I sprinted to the top and now find myself looking at the other side, unable to see how the next half of my life is supposed to measure up.

Is the best yet to come, or has it already passed me by? Did I make too many mistakes and fail too many times for new dreams to be possible? What if all those opportunities I had were because of the connections I had, the people I knew, the title I was given—and now that those things are gone, so are my dreams?

But life is not one single bell curve. As I've been praying through this and asking God to help me dream again, I have a new image in my mind. Life is an endless string of hills—some that take a long time to climb and others that we can ascend in a single step. God, in His goodness, has kept me focused on the climb that is right in front of me until I'm ready to tackle what comes next. And when I view the descent as an opportunity to rest and recover—or maybe to connect with someone along the way whom I can teach what I've just learned so they can start their next climb—I can find contentment in the entire journey, not just in reaching the summit.

God still has work for us to do, and we still have the time and ability to dream big. But if we spend our time watching what everyone else is doing, we'll forget how to hear what God wants us to do. And it's not just secular media and culture telling us what we should have done by now (graduated from college, landed our dream job, bought a house, started a family), but we hear it from faith circles as well. For example, *Relevant* has a list of 20 things people should do before they turn 40—things like seeing your favorite band in concert (not a bad idea), reading the entire Bible (still good), and running a marathon or other race (no thanks).[1]

All of us have watched other people achieving their dreams while we feel stuck. It can be hard when everyone around you is excited to set goals for the new year and all you can think about is the *one* dream you're still waiting on. As much as we want to celebrate and be there for the women in our lives, it can be painful to hear their good news, opportunities, and achievements while we're still wondering why we can't get a *yes* for our first step.

Psalm 34:18 reminds us, "The LORD is near the brokenhearted; he saves those crushed in spirit." God knows our dreams, goals, heartaches, and disappointments. He also knows more than we could ever imagine. He sees what the waiting will accomplish, how we'll grow and be ready when He finally says "yes," and what we need, not just what we want.

You aren't a failure if you haven't achieved all your dreams by now, and God is not done with you yet. He's still at work, and you can still dream.

When our daughter started taking swimming lessons three years ago, she was a natural. In fact, she has excelled at almost everything she has ever tried. She's smart, funny, athletic, and creative. So we weren't surprised when she passed level 1 of swimming on the first try and level 2 with flying colors. At the end of each week she started to expect an ice pop and a little card congratulating her on her accomplishment.

And then came level 3.

For two summers we watched her learn and execute every single move required of her—except one. The whip kick. Whether it was because she learned it wrong the first time, inherited my husband's lack of flexibility, or simply had it in her head that it was too hard and she couldn't do it, it was the one thing that kept her from passing, over and over again. We started to dread Fridays, because not even a Popsicle could overcome the disappointment we knew was coming. Over and over she saw someone else in her class earn their card—and she didn't. I've learned to handle my own struggles with achieving my dreams, but it's something else to watch someone you love feel so discouraged week after week, year after year.

No matter how many times we praised everything our daughter was doing well, she still focused on the one thing she couldn't do. Instead of focusing on all she had accomplished, she dwelled on where she should be by now, failing to recognize her actual ability and believing the lies that she would never figure it out, that she was a terrible swimmer, that she couldn't do anything right.

Sound familiar? Maybe you've gone down that trail before too. You have a dream that you are desperate to accomplish and, until now, everything has come easily. You were surprised when you hit a wall with this goal, but you have pushed forward and keep trying. It feels like you're in the middle of one of those mud runs where everyone around you has a team of people helping to pull them up and over a big, slippery wall, while you're stuck at the bottom by yourself, trying desperately to grab a rope, a ledge, anything that will help you get to the top. You're tired, messy, close to tears. Other runners are saying encouraging words to you as they race by, but you can barely hear them over the noise in your head that shouts that you can't do it. You're not strong enough. You're not smart enough. You're not good enough. You should just give up.

We will never achieve what God has planned for us if we give in to the doubts the world shouts at us. Sometimes we need to be humble enough to ask for help. During Madi's most recent week of swimming lessons, she had an instructor who saw her potential. Although it was hard for Madi to accept extra help, she committed to showing up early for a short private lesson before her swimming class to focus on the whip kick. There were tears, frustrations, and doubts—but she pushed through. She believed us when we told her that her instructors cared about her so much that they wanted to see her succeed, even though it was hard for her to believe it for herself. We watched her put in the work in the pool and practice at home for an entire week—and then it was Friday. Test time.

The smile on her face when she came home with her card stretched from ear to ear. She passed! She felt more joy achieving something that felt impossible than she ever did in the easy levels. It became a highlight of her summer, one of the top three things she shared about when anyone asked her what she did over her school break.

We can always learn something from the dreams that come easily for us, but when we prove to ourselves that we are women who can do hard things—that we won't give up or give in and that it's okay to ask for help—we will be able to persevere through the next obstacle life throws our way. Or as the apostle Paul puts it…

> We have also obtained access through him by faith into this grace in which we stand, and we rejoice in the hope of the glory of God. And not only that, but we also rejoice in our afflictions, because we know that affliction produces endurance, endurance produces proven character, and proven character produces hope. This hope will not disappoint us, because God's love has been poured out in our hearts through the Holy Spirit who was given to us (Romans 5:2-5).

Dreams achieved are worth celebrating, but endurance, character, and hope will be the foundation that we can build the rest of our lives upon as we move forward in confidence toward whatever God has for us.

Digging Deeper

> It was not you who sent me here, but God.
>
> GENESIS 45:8

Joseph's story is an encouraging example of how God's plans are better than our own, even when we don't understand what is going on. Joseph had dreams—literally—about what God had promised to do in his life, but I doubt the path to get there looked anything like he'd hoped. And yet, because of Joseph's love for God, he served and worked humbly, honoring God with his actions. And in the end, Joseph saw how God kept His promises.

Along the way, Joseph connected with people, used his talents, and grew into the man God knew he would become. When we rush to make our plans and dreams happen in our own time, we often miss the opportunities God gives us to learn, grow, and connect.

Joseph's story takes place in the final section of the book of Genesis. He was the youngest son in his family, his father's favorite—and his brothers hated him for it. Jealousy can keep us so focused on what others are doing and what we don't have that we waste time watching someone else's dream instead of pursuing our own.

One day, Joseph excitedly shared a dream he'd had with his family. "Listen to this dream I had: There we were, binding sheaves of grain in the field. Suddenly my sheaf stood up, and your sheaves gathered around it and bowed down to my sheaf" (Genesis 37:6-7). His brothers were, well…less than thrilled. "Are you really going to reign over us?" they asked him. "Are you really going to rule us?" (verse 8).

But wait—there's more! In this section of Scripture, we see dreams coming in pairs, the second affirming the first. Joseph had another dream, one where the sun, moon, and 11 stars bowed down to him. Having not learned anything from sharing the previous dream, he rushed to tell his family. They were angry, again, to learn that Joseph was dreaming that one day his brothers and parents would bow to him (see verses 9-10).

It's encouraging to know that pursuing what God is doing in our lives may not always be comfortable for those around us, but we can still move forward confidently—trusting that we can never make too many mistakes, veer too far off course, or get too distracted to ruin the plans God has made. But we can also learn about timing from Joseph as we discover what and when to share with wisdom and grace, taking into consideration the feelings and reactions of others. Bragging about the amazing opportunity that just fell into your lap may crush the dream of a friend who has been struggling toward that same goal for years. We can love others well when we delight in their pursuit of their passions as we faithfully—and sometimes quietly—take our own next steps.

> **We can love others well when we delight in their pursuit of their passions as we faithfully—and sometimes quietly—take our own next steps.**

We see Joseph's dreams come true more than twenty years later, as his family does bow before him—at least five times![2] But before then, back in the fields when Joseph was still a teenager, his brothers were mad. Like, push-you-into-a-well-and-sell-you-as-a-slave mad. They had this annoying little brother who got all the good clothes and dreamed of ruling over them one day, and they'd had enough. They saw him coming and, in a display of biblical snarkiness, said, "Oh, look, here comes that dream expert!" (verse 19).

So into the well Joseph went. Shortly thereafter, he was sold as a slave to a group of Midianites. From there he made his way to Egypt—certainly not somewhere he probably ever expected to find himself.

But God needed Joseph in Egypt. What we would view as a detour in our dreams, God can use as the road to take us to our new destination, a place we never would have gone had our circumstances stayed the same. I thought being fired from a corporate job I loved was the end of my story, but God used it as a catalyst to move me closer to Him and closer to the work He had for me in ministry.

The doors that feel closed right now, the opportunities that aren't knocking—what if they weren't blocking your progress but giving you a chance to rest, connect, and prepare? God placed Joseph in Egypt, where he needed to be for those first dreams to come true. But Joseph would do more than impact his own family. Ultimately, he would save all Egypt from famine.

In those moments when life feels disappointing, Joseph is an excellent example to follow. He didn't feel sorry for himself. He didn't blame anyone else. He chose to make the best out of each situation, learning, growing, and believing that having problems isn't a problem.

When Joseph reunited with his brothers, he was no longer the 17-year-old they had pushed into a well. He was nearly 40 years old and a powerful, confident governor of Egypt. The robe of many colors that set him apart as a teenager may have been ruined, but God replaced it with "the royal clothing of a king."[3]

Maybe we have things in our lives that we're clinging tightly to—what makes us feel special and set apart—and we're afraid that if we let them go, we'll be vulnerable and exposed. But we can't put on the new before we rid ourselves of the old, and we serve a God who can swap our dirty, messed-up, ripped rags for the clothes of a King.

Although it may feel like the dream God has given you has been delayed or detoured indefinitely, Joseph's story can be your reminder that God is in control of every event. Like Joseph, you can look back and testify that "it was not you who sent me here, but God" (Genesis 45:8).

Flip the Script

- Flip "You should know what you want for your future" to "God, I love that You know exactly what my life will be like even when the path is still unclear to me."

- Flip "You should be successful by now" to "God, I know that Your timing is perfect and that You define success differently. Help me wait patiently on You."

- Flip "You should give up if you haven't succeeded with that dream yet" to "God, help me embrace the journey and develop endurance as I stay faithful where You have called me."

Reflection / Book Club

When you're reaching for your next goal, that thing that is just a little further and higher than what you've just done, looking back doesn't help you move forward. Looking up does. (See Philippians 3:13-14 and Hebrews 12:1-2.) When you keep your eyes turned to God, you can stay focused on the race He's given you to run, trusting that He will do what He says He will do.

No matter how many mistakes you think you've made, you can still dream big, bold, audacious, God-sized dreams. No matter how late to the game you feel, how many people have already done what you want to do, or even if no one has *ever* done what you dream of doing, when you align your dreams with God's will, you can walk confidently toward the next step He has for you. Choose to say "yes" to contentment and dreaming and "no" to comparison and doubt. Look up, friend.

1. What is a dream you've given up on because you thought it was too late or too many people had already done it?

2. How would you approach your dreams and goals differently if you knew the end result was kingdom growth and not personal gain?

3. What are some practical steps you can take to quiet the shout of should so that you can align your dreams with God's will? Is there someone you can share the journey with, someone who can hold you accountable and offer encouragement?

> *God, we're so grateful that You created us in Your image and that You invite us to join You on this adventure. As we fight discouragement for dreams lost or not yet realized, help us look up to You with a fresh, eternal perspective. We trust You and Your timing, and we ask that any dream or goal we set for ourselves that does not line up with Your plan for our lives fade away so we can focus on what You've created us to do. In Jesus' name, amen.*

Quiet Time

Holy Rest

*God blessed the seventh day and declared it holy, for
on it he rested from all his work of creation.*

GENESIS 2:3

Read Genesis 2:1-3

I'm pretty sure my body is 90 percent coffee. As seasons change
and my schedule shifts, my alarm has been set earlier and earlier to try
to find time to get these words on the page. Anyone who has known
me for even the shortest amount of time will confirm that I am not,
in fact, a morning person. I have a new workout plan I'm supposed to
be following that has the word *morning* in the title, and I usually get
to it around 6:00 p.m. I tried for a year or two to lead a small group
of women online, developing a morning routine that would help us
spend time in God's Word first, but I was really only successful at
designing a cute new coffee mug for the program.

I like sleep. But I'm terrible at resting. Rest is low on my to-do list,
something I'll get to after I've pushed through and done the work; said
"yes" to too many things; and decided that it's a smart idea to work two
jobs, write a book, take a grad class, volunteer, spend half my week at
soccer practices, watch all the episodes of *So You Think You Can Dance*,
and brainstormed another dozen ways to try to make social media
work for me, not against me. Sleep is what happens at the end of the
day when I can't keep my eyes open any longer. But rest is a state of the
heart that finds peace in even the busiest season.

God was so gracious to model His balance of work and rest for us at the very beginning of Scripture. He worked hard and created each piece of our world out of nothing, then took time at the end of each day to delight in His work and celebrate what had been accomplished. Not because His work was finished, but because it was good. And at the end, when the task *was* finished, He rested and called it holy.

God didn't rest because *He* needed it—He modeled it because He knew *we'd* need it. Without that last day as an example, we would push forward and do all the things, all the time, in the name of ministry, and we would burn out. Good work can only be sustained when we take a step away from it and make space for our hands and minds to rest. It's our moment to recharge and reconnect with God, to give Him the glory for the work that has been done and to seek His will for the work to come.

Quiet Quest

Without thinking of what anyone else does or what you think "rest" should look like, write down how you feel most connected to God. What needs to happen to create that space to rest in Him? How does real, restorative rest feel different from a few hours of sleep?

A Light Burden

Come to me, all of you who are weary
and burdened, and I will give you rest.

Matthew 11:28

Read Matthew 11:28-30

We live in a small town in Pennsylvania that has a real issue with traffic jams. Sometimes it's caused by farm equipment, other times it's due to a horse and buggy or a group of Mennonite cyclists. Occasionally it's caused by a herd of cows crossing the street. Country road rage is a thing, you guys.

A friend from college came to my hometown for the first time when she was part of my wedding, and I remember how delighted she was to see cows in *real life*. Maybe growing up in this area, surrounded by corn fields and farmers, has given me a deeper appreciation for today's scripture. The "yoke" Jesus talks about in Matthew 11:29-30 is a wooden harness that attaches an animal to a plow or cart. It's hard work to pull a heavy load.

Our heavy loads—the worries, anxieties, work, family, obligations, and expectations filling up our carts—will wear us down. But Jesus invites us to stop and rest with Him. And when we're ready to move forward, we can leave our burdens with God, choosing instead to learn from Jesus as we pick up the lighter yoke He offers, making our journey easier as we work with Him and let Him guide our path.

Quiet Quest

What burden have you been carrying around, for yourself or someone else, that you need to place before Jesus? Get together with a few friends and talk about those things that weigh you down and keep you from going after what God has planned for your lives. How can you work together to lighten the load or hold one another accountable as you take your burdens and cares to God—and leave them there?

A Smart Goal

*By no means do I count myself an expert in all of this, but I've
got my eye on the goal, where God is beckoning us onward—
to Jesus. I'm off and running, and I'm not turning back.*

PHILIPPIANS 3:13-14 MSG

Read Philippians 3:12-17

When I worked as the assistant vice president of marketing for a local financial institution, my boss taught me to set SMART goals—an acronym to help our team set our sights on achievements that were specific, measurable, achievable, relevant, and timely. Saying that we wanted to be more creative was fine, but that goal didn't meet the criteria. Setting a goal to increase the number of proactive marketing pieces we distributed to our 20-plus locations by 25 percent in the next month checked the boxes. It's easy to confuse goals with wishes, but wishes don't become reality unless we assign actionable steps to get there.

If you haven't picked up on it yet, I love setting goals. But just because we have a goal that is SMART doesn't necessarily mean that it's our best option. We need to add a new qualification to our list:

*Does this goal help me get closer to the place God is calling me?
Will it help me become more like Him and keep me reaching
out to Jesus the way He's reaching out for me?*

We have the incredible opportunity of using our gifts in ways that generations before us never even considered. And with every option, every shout of should, every look behind us to see what someone else is doing, we can find ourselves setting goals that move us forward without moving us closer to God. We need to be willing to set aside our good goals for God's best. That's not just smart—that's real wisdom.

Quiet Quest

Make a list of all the things you would like to do—your goals, dreams, bucket-list tasks. Instead of measuring them against a SMART goal plan, spend time in prayer asking God to reveal how they stack up against His sanctification plan. What is God asking you to let go of so that you can stay focused, keep on the right track, and take off running?

Plans of the Heart

A person's heart plans his way,
but the Lord determines his steps.

PROVERBS 16:9

Read Proverbs 16:9

What did you want to be when you were little? Maybe a ballerina, an astronaut, or an artist? Or maybe you hoped to be the world's first firefighting veterinarian race-car driver? Perhaps you were the child who firmly believed that she would get to be a unicorn when she grew up. When we're little and our imaginations are free to create worlds that don't yet exist, we believe we can be anything.

As adults, we often keep our plans and dreams for the future small, so they fit into our expectations and stay rooted in reality. I've read today's verse before—and always from the perspective of limitations. I can do all the planning I want, but unless God says it's okay, it won't happen. But what if the wisdom King Solomon shares with us isn't that we're to dream smaller, but to believe with our whole hearts that we serve a God who can do more than we could ever imagine?

When our plans for the future stay within the confines of expectations and what others are already doing, we don't have new steps for God to establish in our lives. We replicate the work that we see someone else doing, we follow their steps, and our plans are set in motion. However, instead of doing what has already been done, what would our lives look like if our hearts and imaginations dreamed up something wildly unexpected, and we committed it to the Lord? We wouldn't be able to take credit for the steps we would take or the fulfillment of the plan because we would know and testify that it was only God who got us there.

Quiet Quest

"Wildly unexpected" looks different for each of us. What does it look like for you? What dream is outside your daily routine and doesn't exist in your comfort zone or in the realm of anything you can control or create? Maybe it looks like forgiveness and freedom, or serving somewhere new, or starting that dream business. In the quiet moments you find today, ask God for wisdom as you use your imagination and start dreaming again—and trust Him to plan the path.

Big Talk

Like billowing clouds that bring no rain
is the person who talks big but never produces.

PROVERBS 25:14 MSG

Read Proverbs 25:14

Have you ever worked with someone who made big promises, reminded you constantly about their amazing talent, and made sure you knew they were the expert—but you never actually saw any action to back up their big words? Or maybe you know someone who is incredibly gifted, but they refuse—out of fear or doubt or past failures—to use those gifts.

Today's verse says that someone who is all talk and no action is like a rain cloud with no rain. Empty words produce empty results. Just like plants can't thrive and grow without actual rain coming from the clouds, the people around us can't grow when our words speak louder than our actions. But I think it's important to recognize that we also keep others from thriving when we hold our talents closely and don't share them with the people God has placed in our lives.

There are people in your life who need what God has created you to do. They need your encouragement, teaching, hospitality, and faith to make a real, meaningful difference in their life. We need to push past the walls of pride that we've built for protection, use our gifts, and make space for others to feel safe to use theirs too. We need one another, and we can do so much more for God's kingdom when we put our talents into action—together.

Quiet Quest

If you've never taken a spiritual gifts assessment before, take one today (you can find several online). How do your results line up with your passions and interests? Have there been opportunities to use your gifts recently that you've ignored? As you spend some time quietly processing the *why*, invite God to open your eyes to see where He's asking you to put your faith into action—and one way you can do that this week.

Part 4

Faith

11

I Should Pray More

My college roommate told me I was going to hell because I wasn't Catholic. It had been building, this tension between us, for months. The only reason I was in the apartment with her was because we had a mutual friend who kept us together, but now that friend was studying abroad for a semester. Our glue was gone. Everything started falling apart.

I'm not sure what I expected her to say when I finally asked her to admit what I knew she'd been thinking. I was new at this faith thing, and she was headed in an extreme direction. I didn't know where to begin to defend my faith (and honestly didn't know that was something I would ever need to do), and she had all the answers for hers.

It hurt. A lot. I was naive enough to still believe that both of us saying we were Christians meant that we could belong together in some faith-based circle of trust. Somehow, I thought that sharing love for God would cancel out the humanity that comes with being two college-aged girls headed in opposite directions.

It wasn't a great year.

I have fond memories of my time at a Catholic university, but I also have these extraordinarily painful moments when I remember the loneliness, struggle, and inferiority I felt when it came to my faith in that place. What I thought would be a safe, loving environment to connect with friends became a place of exclusion and hurt. I was told—without question—that it didn't matter if I was a Christian. I wasn't good enough without certain elements of the Catholic faith.

Discovering your identity as a young adult is hard enough. Add in an unexpected list of shoulds for your faith, and you've created a recipe for insecurity, doubt, depression, and loneliness.

Our faith isn't exempt from the shouts of should that we battle every day. As a junior in college, I didn't have the full online sphere to contend with, yet still the noise was so loud. I remember being on AOL Instant Messenger to talk to friends, and I was part of Facebook when it was still a place just for college students. This was new territory, navigating the beginnings of social media—and as much as I wasn't prepared to embrace my faith in real life, I definitely didn't have a plan for my online community.

Before social media, the only people I could compare my faith with were my family members, those I knew at church, and friends I was starting to meet in college. Even then I felt like I'd skipped a day of "How to Be a Christian 101." Apparently, everyone else knew when and how often to read their Bible, but I barely knew where to start. Friends were spending time in prayer, gathering to pray for others, using their Friday nights to worship God, and I didn't know how they knew to do that. Going out with friends made sense. Praying and trying to figure out on my own what it meant to hear from God? That was hard. And confusing. I found myself volunteering with a local youth group at a Presbyterian church but felt like a fraud the entire time.

I couldn't answer any of their questions.

Most of the teenagers knew more than I did.

How was I supposed to be a mentor and spiritual leader when I never had one at their age?

When we focus on what others are doing with their faith, we lose sight of the personal relationship Jesus wants to have with us.

And it's even easier now to catch a glimpse of how others engage their faith. Social media shows us what our quiet time should look like as we scroll through beautifully curated photos full of soft light, cozy blankets, and Bibles with neat handwriting in the margins featuring life-changing revelation learned from the Word at 4:00 a.m.

We read blog posts, articles, and books that tell us how often to read the Bible. We join online communities dedicated to teaching us how and when to be in the Word. We sign up for all the reading plans with the hope that maybe, just maybe, one of these times we'll create a habit that will stick—even if it's not the way God created us to connect with Him.

What happens when our lives don't live up to the practically perfect days everyone else seems to have figured out? And what would it look like if we chose to quiet the shout of should in our faith lives and discovered the personal, beautiful, life-giving relationship God wants to have with us instead of trying to have the relationship *she* has with Him?

I pulled out a chair to sit with some girlfriends at Starbucks one evening, joking about the horrendous screeching noise the chair legs made against the tile floor. Our families were a few minutes away, attending a variety of weekly Bible studies at church, and we had decided to gather over coffee instead. The noisy chair joke was my way of delaying the inevitable.

I knew they were going to ask me how I was doing. And I didn't know how to answer them.

So I deflected the conversation, asking everyone what they were drinking and how their week was going. I sipped my tea slowly as we shared about children, work, and what keeps us grounded when life feels chaotic and overwhelming.

A friend looked me in the eye after I reluctantly shared that I was feeling overwhelmed, burned out, and more than a little burdened by all that I had on my plate. "All those things—are they the best for you to do right now?" she asked me. I had to admit that they were. God was giving me the go-ahead to say "yes" to each of the commitments I was making, and I'm pretty good at listening to my gut when something feels like a "no." It wasn't the actual activities I was struggling with, but the discontentment that was so loud in my head all the time.

I had a sense that I should be doing more. All the activities I was already saying "yes" to weren't enough, especially when it came to my faith. I felt like a fraud when my friends then talked about the way they stay grounded through early morning quiet times, journaling, prayer, and worship. All I could think about was the latest series I had binge-watched on Netflix.

Somehow, 20 years after becoming a Christian, I can still feel like

I've missed out on the basics when I start to list all the things I should be doing.

- *I should pray more.*

- *I should wake up early for an hour of quiet time.*

- *I should be able to hear God more clearly.*

- *I should know what the Bible says about that by now.*

- *I should go to seminary so I can be taken seriously.*

- *I should know what to say when I pray.*

My girlfriends may struggle to wake up for their quiet time, but at least they try. After a few seasons of leading an online group committed to starting our mornings with prayer and Bible study (and failing miserably at it, probably because I had a newborn), I joked that God simply hadn't made me for mornings.

The harder truth is that God didn't necessarily make me a morning person or a night owl. I was choosing to create a lifestyle and habits that didn't work well with waking up early, and I was afraid to change. What if I started to wake up early and pray and still didn't know if I was hearing God or my own voice? What if I tried (again) and failed? What if the next time I was asked to pray at a meeting or with friends, I still sounded foolish?

We finished our drinks and pushed in our squeaky chairs to meet our families at church. None of my friends judged me for not wanting to wake up to pray in the morning. They didn't should on me. They'll love me and invite me out for coffee again, but I also know they won't stop looking me in the eye and encouraging me to take my next best step toward a deeper relationship with God. That's what they care about. Not when I pray, or how, or which room I go to in my house, or how much coffee it will take to get me there. They care about my heart.

It's not just our friends who love us, encourage us, and care about our hearts—God does all these and more. And if there is one thing this heart knows, it's this: The world might shout shoulds at us about the details, but God invited us into relationship.

It's not a question about whether or not we should pray. The Bible is clear about that. We're told to be faithful in prayer (Romans 12:12), to pray on all occasions (Ephesians 6:18), to devote ourselves to prayer (Colossians 4:2), and to pray continually (1 Thessalonians 5:17). When it comes to determining the difference between what we think we should do and what we know God is asking us to do, we need to open God's Word.

If we turn to Google instead of God's Word, we'll find ourselves digging through countless articles on when we should pray and how we should pray. The opinions and options of a well-meaning world will find their way into our brains before we can manage to read even one scripture reminding us that prayer is simply how we're invited to communicate with God.

> The world might shout shoulds at us about the details, but God invited us into relationship.

In the New Testament the most common word for *pray* is *proseuchomai*, which is a combination of Greek words that mean "facing/toward" and "speak out." It's a word that invokes specific intention and covers a variety of types of prayer, including submission, confession, supplication, intercession, praise, and thanksgiving.[1] Prayer is the act of realizing a need and bringing it before God with words, whether spoken aloud, written down, or whispered in your heart.

What would your relationship with God look like if you chose to let go of the burden of all the shoulds on your shoulders and simply said "yes" to talking with God more regularly? Maybe your commute to work is your quiet time after you've dropped off the kids at school and you have 20 minutes to yourself. Or maybe you find intentional time each week to go for a walk, just you and God, where you can find a little silence to think as you praise Him.

Our relationship with God isn't meant to be captured in a perfect social media post. We don't pray for the likes; we don't worship for the shares. We do those things because God has invited us into communion with Him, and we can find abundant joy and contentment when we honor Him with our time, our praise, and or hearts.

Digging Deeper

> When you pray, don't babble like the Gentiles, since
> they imagine they'll be heard for their many words.
> Don't be like them, because your Father knows
> the things you need before you ask him.
>
> MATTHEW 6:7-8

Do you ever wonder if we make things a little too hard on ourselves? We seek complicated answers for simple questions and then find ourselves stuck, like the ball in a Rube Goldberg machine, taking eighty steps to do just one easy task. Prayer can feel like that—unnecessarily complicated and hard to get right. Maybe it's because something as important as prayer feels like it should require a lot of work to get right. We're talking with God; it can't be *that* simple, can it?

Although we could turn to several passages of Scripture for instruction on prayer, Matthew 6 feels like the obvious place to start. It doesn't get much easier than "pray like this" (verse 9).

Matthew, the first book of the New Testament, is considered a historical account of the life of Jesus. This Gospel bridges the Old and New Testaments, sharing God's plan from Genesis to Revelation. Chapter 6 covers instruction from Jesus to the disciples on everything from how to give, how to pray, how to fast, what to do with earthly possessions, and dealing with anxiety.

It feels particularly relevant to read this passage in light of our involvement with social media, smartphones, and other technology that constantly connects us. I wonder if Jesus might have adjusted His teaching in verse 5 to say to us today, "Whenever you pray, you must not be like the hypocrites, because they love to pray on Facebook Live and through Instagram Stories to be seen by people."

Instead, according to verse 6, we're to follow a few easy steps: Go into our room, shut the door, pray to our Father, and keep it simple.

Have you ever found yourself so caught up in the shoulds of it all that you've forgotten that prayer is about meeting privately with God to share with Him what He already knows? This isn't to say that praying with friends and in corporate worship is frowned upon, but the time that we spend one-on-one with God is what will prepare our hearts to lead well in those other moments. This is time that we can spend just with God, where we can pour out our hearts, praise Him, sit quietly before Him, and be ourselves. No fancy words or showmanship required—or wanted. God will be there to meet you, no matter where you seek Him.

And, when we don't know what to say or how to pray, verses 9-13 offer a model:

> Our Father in heaven,
>   your name be honored as holy.
> Your kingdom come.
> Your will be done
>   on earth as it is in heaven.
> Give us today our daily bread.
> And forgive us our debts,
>   as we also have forgiven our debtors.
> And do not bring us into temptation,
>   but deliver us from the evil one.

This prayer is an example of how and what to pray, whether alone or in a group. The model shows honor to God's holiness, submission to His will, and constant dependence on His provision. It also shows us that, to pray for forgiveness of our sins, we must first forgive others.[2]

My model of prayer would often look more like a quick hello, a list of things I'm worried about or wish would happen, maybe a request to change someone else's behavior, and an awkward ending.

I think I like Jesus' version better. Let's dive into it together.

Honor God's Holiness

When we start our conversations with God focused on who He is, we put our relationship in proper perspective. God isn't a mythical vending machine where we say the right words and get the answer we're craving. God is holy. There is no one like Him. He alone is God. His name deserves to be honored first and above all. When we proclaim God's holiness with our mouths, we prepare our hearts to submit to His will instead of expecting a specific response.

Submit to God's Will

Our relationship with God is not intended to be an equal partnership. When our prayers value God's will above our plans, we put that relationship into a proper perspective. God knows all, and He can do more than we could ever ask or imagine (see Ephesians 3:20). Trying to manipulate our circumstances to achieve the outcome we desire is selfish and foolish and shows a lack of trust that God is who He says He is. Our resources are limited, and in our own power we will run out of time, energy, and motivation. God sees beyond our immediate wants into what our lives need to fulfill His purpose on earth, and His limitless resources will supply our every need (see Philippians 4:19).

Depend on God's Provision

I struggle with anxiety. It keeps me from sleeping well at night and from truly enjoying new experiences. I worry about the weather, driving to new places, and whether or not the best is yet to come in my life—or if I've already lived it and lost it. At my most anxious, my prayers are unfocused and uncertain. Quieting the noise of the world feels impossible when my brain is going through a running to-do list. Through my worries, I can't see that prayer is not a waste of time, but the best use of my time.

This doesn't mean that we can't bring all the concerns of our hearts to God. In Matthew 6:25-34 Jesus instructs His disciples to worry less about what will happen tomorrow and focus instead on living in a right relationship with God. The Message says it like this:

Has anyone by fussing in front of the mirror ever gotten taller by so much as an inch? All this time and money wasted on fashion—do you think it makes that much difference? Instead of looking at the fashions, walk out into the fields and look at the wildflowers. They never primp or shop, but have you ever seen color and design quite like it? The ten best-dressed men and women in the country look shabby alongside them.

If God gives such attention to the appearance of wildflowers—most of which are never even seen—don't you think he'll attend to you, take pride in you, do his best for you? What I'm trying to do here is to get you to relax, to not be so preoccupied with *getting*, so you can respond to God's *giving*. People who don't know God and the way he works fuss over these things, but you know both God and how he works. Steep your life in God-reality, God-initiative, God-provisions. Don't worry about missing out. You'll find all your everyday human concerns will be met.

Give your entire attention to what God is doing right now, and don't get worked up about what may or may not happen tomorrow. God will help you deal with whatever hard things come up when the time comes (Matthew 6:27-34).

Don't stress about missing out. God will provide.

Forgive First

Honor God's holiness. Submit to His will. Depend on His provision. Be the first to forgive. Jesus' example for prayer is incredibly countercultural. The world might tell us we should be able to provide for ourselves, carve our own paths, and hold out until the other person apologizes first, but that's not what God asks of us. In His kingdom, putting others first is a reflection of the way He first loved us. If we expect others to show love and forgiveness, it's up to us to be the example and to be humble enough to go first.

Following Jesus' example not only helps us approach the throne of God with humility and honor, but developing a deep and robust prayer life retrains our brains to cut out the noise, comparison, doubt, and distractions that keep us from staying alert to God's will. When our minds are distracted and occupied with all the shoulds, we're not able to pray clearly, with focus.

Whether we start with "Hey, God" like a friend of mine, or we come before Jesus more formally, prayer is our way of communicating with Him—and He wants to hear from us.

Flip the Script

- Flip "You should have a long quiet time every morning" to "God, Your Word tells me to pray without ceasing, and I'm so glad I can talk to You any time of day."

- Flip "You should know how to pray" to "God, thank You for inviting me to come to You just as I am, without any pretense or formalities."

- Flip "You should know how to hear from God" to "God, help me stay close to You and embrace the way You want to speak into my life, whether it's through your Word, music, nature, or something I can't even imagine yet."

Reflection / Book Club

So many parts of our lives get should on, but we often think our faith is immune. In reality, we were never promised that the journey of following Jesus would be struggle-free, and personal growth happens when we're open to the teaching and influence of wise mentors. Unfortunately, we find ourselves bombarded with how-tos; blog posts; well-meaning friends who think their way is right; and a bossy, noisy world that would feel much more comfortable if we all fit into the same box. Discerning the wise from the worldly happens when we're intentional to see what God says—first.

A.W. Tozer said, "Some of the churches now advertise courses on how to pray. How ridiculous! That is like giving a course on how to fall in love."[3] Maybe we don't need courses on how to pray, but as a new Christian, I remember wishing I did have just one person who could help me navigate what felt like a whole new language.

If you're at the beginning of your journey with Jesus, do you have a close friend, mentor, pastor, or spiritual adviser who can help you learn how to talk to God? If you're more experienced and have some wisdom to share, is there a new Christian in your workplace, church, or community whom you can come alongside to mentor? Dig into God's Word with someone else, learn what His purpose is for prayer, and consider how your season of life, personality, and gifts can come together to create the kind of communion with God that works for *you*.

Today, either on your own or with a study group, take a look at a Bible story about a woman who prayed. You could read Hannah's story in 1 Samuel 1–2, Mary's story in Luke 1, or Anna's story in Luke 2:36-38.

1. What can you learn from this example of prayer?

2. How do you connect with this story?

3. Spend some time in prayer, honoring God for His holiness and seeking His will. You can use the following prayer with your group or work through the example Jesus gave and write or share your own prayer. Pray with confidence, knowing that God not only hears you—He wants to hear from you.

> *Lord, thank You for the example You've given us in Scripture—not just an example of prayer, but of everything we need to be in a relationship with You. You are holy, and we praise You for Your wisdom, faithfulness, and mercy. As we seek to quiet the shout of should in our lives, help us hear Your soft, still voice so we can be women of faith who say "yes" to You, leaning in with holy anticipation of what You're about to do in us and through us. We love You, Lord. In Jesus' name, amen.*

12

I Should Never Doubt What God Has Planned for Me

I never saw myself growing older.

I could always imagine what I would be like in college and what I would achieve, and even as a young adult I could picture my career, but I never once allowed myself to think of what life beyond 30 would look like. Realistically, I know that the next half of my life holds as much promise as the first half—maybe even more. But if you ask me to describe what I'm working toward, hoping for, praying about, I wouldn't have much to tell you. Am I allowed to doubt that God still has plans for me?

It doesn't take much social-media scrolling or Etsy-shop searching to find artwork encouraging us to be strong and courageous, a reminder from Joshua 1:9 that God is with us wherever we go: "Haven't I commanded you: be strong and courageous? Do not be afraid or discouraged, for the LORD your God is with you wherever you go." But what if we don't know where we're going? How do we stop to ask for directions when we feel like other believers won't understand? If we share even our smallest doubts about our purpose, direction, or future, will they make us feel like we're doing this faith thing all wrong?

Consider this final chapter your safe place to be as real and honest as you can be with yourself and God. We will never be able to quiet the shouts of should in a sustainable way if we're not willing to dig deep and uncover the reasons why we listen to everyone else but struggle to hear God. Seeds of doubt planted in our hearts—by others or by our-selves—prepare a pathway for the enemy to sneak into our minds and distract us from what God wants to do. When we keep those fears and struggles to ourselves, we give them room to put down roots.

Doubts grow in the dark. Telling other people they should never doubt what God has planned for them closes down opportunities to share our testimony, offer encouragement, study God's Word together, or hold one another accountable. In our lives we will have doubts, but we can help one another overcome them when we stop pretending to be perfect and choose to be works in progress together.

We're so willing to explore our doubts when it comes to our work, goals, hobbies, and even families—but our faith is supposed to be this one perfect, unblemished area of our lives that can't possibly have any-thing wrong with it. What if someone who doesn't believe in God real-izes that we're working through our own questions or sees us struggling to understand prayers that have yet to be answered?

Your doubts are not powerful enough to stop the transforming work of the Holy Spirit in someone else's life, and they certainly aren't going to be big enough to diminish the sacrifice Jesus made for us on the cross. They could, however, invite someone into a conversation who is willing to bring their own mess to the table because they finally found someone who isn't pretending to be perfect. And your own willingness to find the answers to your questions about God's plans for your life, His character, or your identity as His daughter will take you on a journey into a deeper faith than you ever expected.

> In our lives we will have doubts, but we can help one another overcome them when we stop pretending to be perfect and choose to be works in progress together.

In the car the other day our daughter—after asking a string of questions about the different types of lines on the road—made sure to remind us, her exasperated parents, that questions are important because it's how she learns new things. Questions help children understand the world around them, how they fit into it, and how to safely interact with their environment. Do I want to spend time trying to answer questions about gravity, how crayons are made, or where the fabric from her shirt came from? Honestly, not usually. Do I want her to be curious and explore her world, encouraging her interests and helping her stay excited about arts and science? Absolutely.

Our doubts about God's plans for our lives can take us into a deeper relationship with Him if we're willing to bring our concerns into the light and seek His answers to our questions. As we understand more of God's character through studying His Word, we'll find comfort and freedom in learning that we don't need to know His whole plan for us right this second. We'll find peace and encouragement when we celebrate what God has done in the past and trust Him to continue to work in the future.

In an 1855 sermon, Charles Spurgeon said,

> I do not believe there ever existed a Christian yet, who did not now and then doubt his interest in Jesus. I think, when a man says, "I never doubt," it is quite time for us to doubt him, it is quite time for us to begin to say, "Ah, poor soul, I am afraid you are not on the road at all, for if you were, you would see so many things in yourself, and so much glory in Christ more than you deserve, that you would be so much ashamed of yourself, as even to say, 'It is too good to be true.'"[1]

The enemy wants us to believe that we're the only women of faith who have ever doubted. That belief will keep our hearts closed off, ashamed of our questions instead of living in awe of a God who knows our sins and our mess and loves us more than we deserve. The more we recognize the greatness of our sin, the more we are overwhelmed by the glory and goodness of God. And the closer we walk with Him, the more His light shines on the things we want to keep hidden—which can either bring us to our knees in need of our Savior or harden our hearts as we strive to keep our sins buried.

> **Celebrate what God has done in the past and trust Him to continue to work in the future.**

There will be seasons when we have absolutely no idea what God is doing, and we doubt our direction, profession, and next steps. It's okay to ask Him the hard questions and share your doubts and fears. Share your struggles with friends who can encourage and pray for you. Ask God to help you use this season as an opportunity to grow closer to Him, to get to know Him better. Then, when the time comes that He reveals the next step or opens the door you've been waiting for, you'll not only be alert and prepared, but stronger in your faith than ever before.

We sat on a stone patio outside of an orphanage in Ensenada, Mexico, as the sun came up. The kids were all still asleep, including the members of the high school youth group we had with us from Pennsylvania. The culture shock was real, but so was the absolute love those teenagers showed to every kid they met. Through art and soccer, painting walls and worshiping together, they bonded over things that didn't need translation.

Surrounded by rising sunlight and almost absolute quiet, exhausted from traveling, serving, mentoring, poor attempts at communicating, and feeling completely homesick, I was overcome. A friend sat reading a devotional beside me and, when she saw my emotions, didn't stop reading but started to read out loud.

God and I connect most deeply when I'm the most vulnerable, when I'm too worn out to keep up the facade of control, and when I finally put myself in a situation where the quiet is louder than the to-do list or the shoulds running through my head. It's in those rare times when I know that what I hear and feel is from the Holy Spirit, instead of doubting and wondering if I'm giving myself the answer.

As my friend read her devotional and prayed for me, I wept. It's what happens when I feel God near, all my emotions bubbling over as I let down my guard, and I can count on both hands the number of times I've created the space to allow it to happen. It happened when I was 16 and became a Christian. It happened when we lost our first pregnancy. It happened during worship, when my heart was so moved by the music and connection to the Holy Spirit that everything else seemed to fall away.

I'm not uncomfortable in silence, not the way most people are. I don't feel the need to fill the empty space in conversations with words, and if someone needs a moment to think about what they want to share, that's fine with me. I can ask questions to a group when I'm speaking and stand quietly at the front of the room until someone answers without feeling awkward or nervous. But the rare moments when I'm alone with my thoughts, when the world is quiet and the distractions are taken away—that's what makes me uncomfortable. It's also when I can be most authentically myself, vulnerable without anyone watching to see if I will make a mistake.

Who am I when the world is quiet, and I can truly hear God? What might He ask me to do if I create the space to truly hear His answer? What might He ask me to give up, an idol that has become more important in my life? What doubts might rise to the surface? Will I feel like an impostor, coming before the throne of Jesus?

Living our best life has nothing to do with wearing a cute outfit from the Nordstrom sale at the newest restaurant in town and capturing it for Instagram. It has everything to do with coming before God with our mess, doubts, dreams, sins, and struggles. God, who sent His one and only Son to come and die for us, doesn't want us to live in the dark, buried under the weight of the world's shoulds. He wants us to step into the light, into freedom and forgiveness. He doesn't want our perfect Valentine's Day–shaped hearts. He wants us to invite Him into the beat-up, broken, scared, and scarred hearts that desperately need His perfect love.

Quieting the shout of should will be uncomfortable. We'll feel vulnerable as we lay down the armor the world has given us and embrace who God has made us to be—women made in His image. We'll unbuckle the belt of opinions that helps us fit in easily and take on the belt of truth that sets us apart and, occasionally, makes us unpopular. We'll remove the breastplate of self-righteousness that gives us a false sense of security and trade it for the breastplate of righteousness that values justice. Instead of putting on running shoes that prepare us to fight or flee, we'll stand firm in shoes built from the peace of the gospel. It is not with our sharp words or quick wit that we'll protect ourselves, but with a shield of faith and the Word of God.

We are works in progress who need a village to help us navigate every season into which God brings us. We are women who seek to swap expectations for joy, insecurities for peace, clutter for creativity, obligation for freedom, quantity for quality, empty words for empathy, worry for wonder, paralysis for progress, and comparison for contentment.

God wants us to invite Him into the beat-up, broken, scared, and scarred hearts that desperately need His perfect love.

My challenge for you, before you move on to the next book, is to create the space to encounter God in the quiet. I'm not going to tell you what that should look like, how long it should take, where you should do it, or even what time of day you should choose. Find the quiet. Shut the door on what the world is shouting at you and come before God with your whole heart. Be open to the opportunity to be vulnerable before Him and listen. Be still.

> The LORD your God is in your midst,
>   a Warrior who saves.
> He will rejoice over you with joy;
> He will be quiet in His love
>   [making no mention of your past sins],
> He will rejoice over you with shouts of joy
>   (Zephaniah 3:17 AMP).

Digging Deeper

> Daniel distinguished himself above the administrators
>   and satraps because he had an extraordinary spirit, so
> the king planned to set him over the whole realm. The
> administrators and satraps, therefore, kept trying to find
> a charge against Daniel regarding the kingdom. But they
> could find no charge or corruption, for he was trustworthy,
>   and no negligence or corruption was found in him.
>
> DANIEL 6:3-4

There is no better place to turn when we're struggling with doubt than to Scripture. These God-breathed words give us hope, comfort, and encouragement as we remember all that God has done and what He promises to do in the future. When our circumstances feel impossible, when we're struggling to be in the world but not adapt to it, stories like Daniel's are there to remind us that God is sovereign over all, and He will be victorious.

The book of Daniel is believed to have been written by Daniel in the years following his captivity in Babylon, where he ministered between 605 BC and around 538 BC. Born into a royal family and taken prisoner when Babylon defeated Jerusalem, Daniel and his friends probably would have been 15 or 16 years old when they were captured. Considered "without any physical defect, good-looking, suitable for instruction in all wisdom, knowledgeable, perceptive, and capable of serving in the king's palace" (Daniel 1:4), these young men would be trained and brought up in the Babylonian culture with the expectation that they would influence others to acclimate to their new way of life, instead of fighting or fleeing.

As a reflection of their new culture, the young men were given new names. Their Hebrew names were rich in meaning. The name Daniel means "God is my judge." Hananiah means "Yahweh is gracious." Mishael means "Who is like God?" And Azariah means "Yahweh is my helper." Their new names—Belteshazzar, Shadrach, Meshach, and Abednego, respectively—acknowledged the Babylonian deities Bel, Aku, and Nego.[2] Although Ashpenaz, Nebuchadnezzar's chief eunuch, changed their names, gave them new clothes, and immersed them in a new culture, the hearts of these faithful young men could not be changed.

This situation is a familiar one to believers today. As Raechel Myers puts it,

> The world will try to rename you your entire life. You'll call yourself "Christian," and the world will call you a square. God calls you "brand new," and the world will try to tell

you you're stuck where you are. God writes "redeemed" across your forehead, and the broken world will try six days from Sunday to make you forget it. But you know, because God's Word tells you, that your "citizenship is in heaven" (Php 3:20). Let the One who made you also name you, and let that be the only name you'll ever need.[3]

As we dive into Daniel's story, we discover that we can trust God, even when everything we know and love is taken away. When we're faced with trials and we feel alone, we can believe that God will be with us. And when the world presses in from every side, we can stand firm in our faith—loving others well, treating one another with respect, and living counterculturally.

Daniel navigated the challenges presented to him with wisdom and favor from God. The obedience and faith of Daniel and his friends resulted in God's blessing, even as God was in the process of disciplining His people. As one commentary puts it, "Daniel demonstrates that the battle for holiness is either won or lost in the small areas of life. Instead of attempting to change circumstances that are beyond his control, he shifts his focus to simply obeying God."[4] Daniel's obedience to God doesn't just benefit him—it makes his supervisor look good, spares a group of Nebuchadnezzar's advisers from death (see Daniel 2), and leads to influencing kings.[5] Daniel was willing to be a work in progress, shaped by God under seemingly impossible circumstances into a man who would stand with Jesus in the lion's den.

Even as Daniel was faced with challenges and tasks that he knew were beyond his abilities, God honored his faithful obedience. When God revealed the true message behind Nebuchadnezzar's dream in

Daniel 2, Daniel worshiped God before running to deliver the message to the king.

> May the name of God
>> be praised forever and ever,
>> for wisdom and power belong to him.
> He changes the times and seasons;
>> he removes kings and establishes kings.
> He gives wisdom to the wise
>> and knowledge to those
>> who have understanding.
> He reveals the deep and hidden things;
>> he knows what is in the darkness,
>> and light dwells with him.
> I offer thanks and praise to you,
> God of my fathers,
>> because you have given me
>> wisdom and power.
> And now you have let me know
>> what we asked of you,
>> for you have let us know
>> the king's mystery (verses 20-23).

Nebuchadnezzar was impressed and God was at work, putting everything into motion to place Daniel and his friends in positions of power and influence. Although the Babylonian king seemed to miss the entire point of the dream revelation, the result—Daniel's friends' refusal to worship the king's giant gold statue, the sentencing of the Hebrew men to death in a fiery furnace, and their miraculous survival—was used to change Nebuchadnezzar's heart (3:13-30).

Now it is Nebuchadnezzar who praises God and acknowledges His eternal kingdom and rule over all the earth—a change of heart that only becomes a permanent change after God takes everything away, including his pride. Once humbled, God restores Nebuchadnezzar to his position of power in Babylon, blessing him even more than before because of his devotion to the one true King (see Daniel 4).

The book of Daniel is full of examples of God's sovereignty over all circumstances, kingdoms, and rulers. From surviving fires to being saved from lions, being blessed with special gifts to being placed in positions of influence, not one moment of Daniel and his friends' time in captivity was wasted. God used every moment and every challenge to bring more people into relationship with Him, through the faithful obedience of four Hebrew men. Where Daniel wasn't yet equipped, he asked, and God provided.

Not only can we look at the story of Daniel and be encouraged as we stand firm against a culture that wants us to conform and fit in, but we can stop striving in our efforts to be perfect as we share the gospel and simply be who God created us to be—works in progress who need God to fill in where we lack so He can get the honor and glory. There is no doubt that God has a plan for your life. Make room for Him to work it out in and through you—even if it goes against what everyone around you is expecting.

Flip the Script

- Flip "You should know what your calling is" to "God, I know that You have a plan for my life, even if I don't know all the details yet."

- Flip "You should keep your doubts to yourself" to "God,

being honest with others helps me give You the glory as I show my dependence on You."

- Flip "You should always know what your next step should be" to "God, sometimes the path feels really unclear, but I will keep following You until You show me the way."

Reflection / Book Club

Quieting the shout of should is hard. It takes intentional effort every day to identify the areas that are pulling us away from God and make small changes to turn back to Him. It takes courage and hard work, but at the end of our lives, I hope we can each hear that precious "Well done, good and faithful servant!" (Matthew 25:21).

Your life might be the very example someone else needs for permission to say "no" to the shoulds of the world and "yes" to what God has designed for them—their best life. That's a big responsibility, and one I'm so grateful we can tackle together. Know that I am cheering for you, but more than that, I'm praying for you. I'm praying that God would surround you with women who will offer encouragement, support, correction, laughter, discipline, and prayer so that you would be able to hear God over the shouts of the world. I'm praying for a community who is *for* you, for precious times with God in places you might never expect, and for you to believe with your whole heart that God loves you, has a plan and purpose for you, and is not done with you yet.

1. Are you afraid to admit that you occasionally have doubts about God's plan for your life? What would need to happen for you to share those doubts with someone else?

2. As you look back over the shoulds we've discussed in the book, is there one in particular that stands out to you? What small steps will you take to quiet that should in your life?

3. How can you use what you've learned and what God has revealed to you on these pages to encourage another woman to embrace who God has made her to be?

God, thank You for the opportunity to go on this journey. We are in awe of all You are, rejoice over all You have done, and wait with joyful expectation for all You will do. May living our best life mean making Christ greater and ourselves less so that others might see You in all we do and say. Give us courage to follow You, strength to pull away from the temptations of the world, and grace as we share the story You're writing for our lives with others. In Jesus' name, amen.

Quiet
Time

In Everything

*Don't worry about anything, but in everything, through prayer
and petition with thanksgiving, present your requests to God.*

PHILIPPIANS 4:6

Read Philippians 4:6–7

I overthink things. I replay conversations, wondering if there was a deeper meaning behind someone's words. I imagine discussions and disagreements that haven't happened yet, planning what I would say so that I'm prepared and not overly emotional when the time comes. I worry and battle anxiety, and when things feel rocky or uncertain, I retreat—and then wonder why I feel lonely.

We all worry about things that we care about. We're concerned about the health of a loved one, and we feel anxious before the job interview we've been working toward. These are feelings that represent our compassion, empathy, and anticipation. Those are good things that remind us that we're humble and human and have kind hearts. But like any emotion, it's not how we feel that is the issue—it's the action we take because of it.

When we choose to go to God in prayer with thanksgiving, bringing all our big feelings and concerns to Him, we're showing that we trust Him. When we overthink the details and act out of a place of fear, we're leaning into the world shouting that we should be able to manage this on our own, instead of having faith that God is with us every step of the way. By presenting every request, every detail of our day to God and remaining close to Him through prayer, we'll be able to see

His hand at work in our lives—and that's something for which we can be thankful.

Quiet Quest

If you're a morning person, set your alarm a little earlier so you're able to wake up to watch the sunrise. If, like me, you're not a morning person, set a reminder on your phone to go outside and watch the sunset. In the quiet, use these moments as a reminder that each day begins and ends without any input from us. We can't worry a new day into existence, and we can't make the sun set any earlier than it does. Thank God for all He has done in your life and bring those cares and worries before Him. He wants to hear from you, and He has time for you.

Be Quiet

The LORD will fight for you, and you must be quiet.

EXODUS 14:14

Read Exodus 14:13-14

Did you know that three children in the back seat of a car can make so much noise that you can't hear yourself think? We spent the weekend visiting my sister and decided to take our daughter and her two cousins back-to-school shopping, which meant a 20-minute drive on the highway to get to our favorite stores. My sister and I were trying to figure out how we could fit more coffee into our morning as the three small humans in the back seat laughed, talked, and played a game at a volume approximately 12 levels up from "outside voice."

You know those glass dividers taxis have? I've never wanted one more. Especially when the giggles turned to questions from all directions about how long it would be until we got there and what we would buy and what we would do if the store didn't have something that would match and if we could go do this thing five hours from now because we must plan our entire day before the actual day has even started.

When Moses looked at the Israelites, who were frankly serving him some serious sarcasm and attitude, and told them, "The LORD will fight for you, and you must be quiet" (Exodus 14:14), all the mamas said, "Amen." Although my sister and I were happy to answer every question the kids were asking (most of them, anyway), they couldn't hear anything we were saying because they kept talking. How often do we do that to God? We come before Him with questions or concerns and never stop or remain quiet enough to hear God's answer—or leave room for Him to do the work He's promised to do.

God had a plan for the people of Israel. They just needed to be still, be quiet, and have faith even when their circumstances felt confusing and hard. God said He would fight for them, and He did. And He will part the seas in your life too.

Quiet Quest

How comfortable are you with silence? The next time you have a conversation with a friend or someone in your family, pay attention to the moments between the words. Do you try to quickly fill the silence, or are you comfortable sitting in that space for a while? How much deeper does your conversation go when you slowly count to ten before jumping in to speak, creating space for the other person to process or respond? What can be said in the quiet that our words could never communicate?

In God Alone

Rest in God alone, my soul,
for my hope comes from him.

PSALM 62:5

Read Psalm 62:5-7

I'm not good at waiting. My husband is fond of reminding me that some results require a process when I'm feeling impatient that things aren't coming together in my expected timeline. I would rather push ahead, work around, step over, and skip a few steps to get to the end. Especially when the process is hard or painful.

Do good things come to those who wait? According to today's scripture, great things come to those who choose to rest in God alone. In Him we find hope and salvation. When those challenging times come and our world feels shaken, He is a firm foundation, our rock and our stronghold. Everything depends on God, and we can trust Him at all times and in all things.

Rest and waiting are good skills to develop, but nothing will bring glory and salvation to our lives other than God. When we find that deep, restorative, soul-rest in God—the kind that draws us into His presence and strengthens our relationship with Him—we can face any process, trial, task, hurdle, opportunity, or hurt with hope. He is our refuge, and we can rest and wait in Him.

Quiet Quest

What do you need to do differently to transform your moments of waiting into moments of resting in God alone? What do your feelings about waiting or taking time to rest reveal about the depth of your trust in God? What are you afraid might happen if you stop trying to control the waiting? Find a moment today to simply sit in the presence of God and rest.

Follow Me

My sheep hear my voice, I know them, and they follow me.

JOHN 10:27

Read John 10:27-29

Have you ever been in a crowded room and heard someone call your name? Somehow, you heard them over the chatter and noise of everyone else talking. You knew, even though there was surely someone else in the room with the same name, that this person was calling *you*. Maybe it was a friend, a coworker, or a family member, and some part of your brain recognized that you knew their voice.

Today's verse paints a beautiful picture of what it looks like to have a relationship with Jesus. Over the shouts of the world and the chaos that distracts us, when we know Him—really know Him—and spend time in the Word and quiet our hearts to be able to hear what He speaks into our lives, we can recognize His voice. Jesus calls for us, and we respond by following Him. We know it's safe, and He will lead us in a direction that ultimately brings us home.

The enemy wants us to stay focused on all that's happening around us—comparing ourselves to others, trying to keep up, striving to check all the boxes and be the perfect Christian/wife/mother/sister/friend/coworker. In our distraction we struggle to focus our attention on Jesus. We begin to follow a voice that leads us toward destruction and deception because we don't recognize Jesus' call on our lives.

Lean in. Learn His voice. Follow Him.

Quiet Quest

If you don't already have time dedicated to reading God's Word, how can you begin to incorporate this spiritual discipline into your life? Feel free to be creative and find opportunities that work well in your current season of life, like having your Bible app read you scripture as you drive or signing up to receive a daily scripture text message.

In All Your Ways

Trust in the LORD with all your heart,
and do not rely on your own understanding;
in all your ways know him,
and he will make your paths straight.

PROVERBS 3:5-6

Read Proverbs 3:5-6

On days when I'm starting to listen to the world's shoulds instead of God, I hijack today's scripture.

Trust in *yourself* with all your heart,
and *do* rely *completely* on your own understanding;
in all your ways know *yourself*,
and *you* will make your paths straight.

Instead of acknowledging God in all things, giving Him credit for what is happening in my life and trusting Him to guide my steps, I make it all about me. My pride begins to get in the way of serving others, and I start wondering why I'm not included, why that happened without me, how I could make myself known in that situation. I want the recognition, and when I don't receive it, when my work is done without any accolades or fanfare, I question my value and identity.

On the other hand, when my life is centered around knowing God, trusting Him, and relying on Him to set the path and lead me on it, my security and worth are unshakable. In the quiet moments when the work is finished and it is good, I can give God the glory—and that's more than enough. When I acknowledge Him in every area of my life and credit Him for the hope, peace, grace, and love that others receive from me, I can find joy in faithful obedience and the encouragement to press forward.

Wherever you were when you started this journey, my prayer is that you turn the last page of this book with a renewed desire to know Jesus more. His quiet whisper will change your life in ways you can't even imagine—more significantly than any shout of should ever will.

Quiet Quest

Worship God today and thank Him for taking you on this journey. Ask Him to show you where you've made yourself the hero of the story and then step aside, believing that He will not leave you, forsake you, or take you down the wrong path.

Appendix

Women Who Silenced Should

What if we took a look at women who silenced should—not to compare ourselves to their lives or to try to be more like them, but to be encouraged to live true to who God made *us* to be? The following are real-life women who went first, stood up for what they believed in, and silenced the shouts of should so they could be difference makers.

As you read their stories, pay attention to the women in your life who are modeling this as well. Who is going against current culture to show someone what it looks like to be a true friend? Who is prioritizing their time with God over adding more to their to-do list? Who is saying "yes" to the job that never existed before, the role that has never been an option before, or the path that is unfamiliar but so right for them?

This is my challenge for you: Honor them. Be a woman who see the best qualities in someone else and calls it out. Encourage their decisions, support their ideas, pray for their endurance. What we do, day to day, may never show up in a history book—but the choices we make to quiet the shouts of should and embrace who God made us to be will make a difference in the lives of those around us.

Tommy Tompkins

It took four days before anyone realized that Gertrude "Tommy" Tompkins was missing. Tompkins was a World War II aviator from New Jersey, a member of the Women Airforce Service Pilots (WASPs).

WASPs flew planes across oceans for delivery, tested new planes, and trained other pilots. More than 25,000 women applied for the WASPs, and less than 2,000 were accepted. "All of these women provided a great service to their country during a time of war, but even more so to the generations of women who would follow their path."[1]

By the time Tompkins went missing, somewhere between leaving what is now Los Angeles International Airport and New Jersey, flying a brand-new plane to its scheduled destination, she had flown more than 750 hours. Of the 38 WASPs who lost their lives in World War II, Tompkins is the only one who has yet to be found.[2]

Tompkins' story is a remarkable account, not only because she was a woman who silenced the "should" of her generation that told her women weren't cut out to do those kinds of jobs, but because she overcame personal obstacles. The first time she flew a P-51 fighter was also the first time the stutter she struggled with her entire life went away, and she pursued her dreams even after losing her first love. Tompkins joined a group of women committed to playing their part in history.

Tompkins serves as a reminder that the decisions we make may not put us in the spotlight. In fact, quieting the shout of should is often less about the accolades we'll receive in our lifetime and more about the opportunities we have to open a door for someone else, making it a little easier for the next woman or the next generation to step into the role God has designed for them.

Ada Lovelace

What if all your best ideas, creations, and dreams were never recognized publicly in your lifetime? Would you still pursue them? Would you still study, write, paint, sing, and work quietly, with faith that God had a plan for the things He created you to do? We live in a time when great works must be recognized publicly in significant ways the second they're made available to the public, or they're not considered a success. Bestseller lists, music charts, release-day ticket sales, viral videos—it's all so loud and bossy and shouts at us that our success and legacy are dependent on the opinions and pocketbooks of others.

It took more than 100 years for Ada Lovelace's contributions to the scientific world to be discovered and appreciated. "Considered to be the first computer programmer," Lovelace learned math and science as a child because her mother did not want her to grow up to be like her father (whom her mother had divorced), Lord Byron.[3]

We're much more familiar with the names of the men Lovelace knew—names like Michael Faraday (known for creating the Faraday cage and the electric motor) and Charles Dickens (author of well-known stories like *Oliver Twist* and *A Christmas Carol*). Even today, their online biographies go into triple the details of their accomplishments and achievements, while Lovelace's life is wrapped around the lives of the men she knew, men she didn't want to be, and the men who helped her.

In addition to learning from a social reformer and a family doctor, Lovelace also had the opportunity to study with "Mary Somerville, a Scottish astronomer and mathematician. Somerville was one of the first women to be admitted into the Royal Astronomical Society." Lovelace's aristocratic status gave her the opportunity to continue her mathematical studies, and in 1843 she translated an article for a scientific journal about the work of one of her mentors, adding her own comments and theories—contributions to the future field of computer science that were finally recognized in the 1950s.[4]

Lovelace, her mother, and teachers like Somerville silenced the shout of should in an era that said education, science, and math were only for men. Lovelace used her gifts to advance the world in ways she would never live to see or even understand in her lifetime. The phone you have in your hand, the computer used to write this book, the next technological invention that we have yet to discover—it all started with the brilliant mind of a young British woman who theorized computer coding (a topic my daughter now reads about in fiction books at bedtime).

Quieting the shout of should is not dependent on age, stage of life, or wealth. It's a mindset we choose each day that is equally content with who God created us to be and discontent when we aren't living with purpose. Quieting the shout of should isn't about settling for less, but about setting our focus on fully living the abundant life God has designed for us.

Kristen Welch

True hospitality doesn't just happen inside the walls of our homes; it's something we take out into the world. In 2010, Kristen Welch traveled to Africa with Compassion International, a humanitarian aid organization that helps children living in poverty by partnering them with sponsors around the world. Welch was heartbroken to learn about the number of girls who were having dangerous backstreet abortions, forced into prostitution, and abandoned by their families. She also met a young woman named Maureen who had graduated from the Compassion leadership program. Maureen Kaderi changed the lives of more than a thousand children simply by sharing her story with potential sponsors.

While the world may have shouted at Welch that she was already doing enough, God had another plan. One that would keep Welch and Kaderi connected from Africa to America as they prayed for months about what they could do to help those girls in danger. The answer? Rehema House—a safe place for young women to go where they would be welcomed and cared for during and after their pregnancy.

Welch utilized her network of friends, online community, and supporters to raise the funds needed for her nonprofit organization, Mercy House Global, to make Rehema House a reality. Kaderi leaned into the education and leadership skills God had given her to manage Rehema House. From Kenya to Texas, these women have silenced the shouts that they should let someone else do the work, and they have discovered that inviting people into your life can change their lives—and yours—forever.

And now? Rehema House consists of two maternity homes where they offer prenatal and postnatal care, education, an opportunity to learn life and vocational skills, and spiritual development and counseling.[5] Also, Welch realized the need to "empower [the girls'] families with dignified jobs so that we could help break the cycle of generational poverty."[6] The launch of "Fair Trade Friday" has given women around the world an opportunity to earn an income. In Texas, Welch invites others into their lives to help as volunteers, packing the fair-trade products for buyers.

What started as a trip to Africa in 2010 has changed the lives of thousands of women around the world because one woman was willing to say "yes" when God asked her to redefine hospitality and open the doors of Mercy House to His daughters.

Learn more about how you can support the work of Mercy House Global at mercyhouseglobal.org.

Wangari Maathai

Have you ever wished you could do something to make a difference in the world but didn't know where to start? What if it took just one small idea to start something that would impact the entire world? For Wangari Maathai, that idea was trees. Planting trees, specifically, as part of her work on environmental conservation. Born in 1940 in rural Kenya, Maathai became "the first woman in East and Central Africa to earn a doctorate degree," which she received from the University of Nairobi, having previously earned degrees from Mount Saint Scholastica College in Atchison, Kansas, and the University of Pittsburgh in Pennsylvania.

Her list of accomplishments is impressive and extensive, from a Nobel Peace Prize (she was the first African woman to win one) to an appointment as a United Nations Messenger of Peace. At the root of those awards, recognitions, titles, degrees, and positions was a woman passionate about "poverty reduction and environmental conservation through tree planting."[7] Her idea—that village women could slow deforestation, create fuel sources, have clean drinking water, build shelters, and improve the environment by planting trees—became a movement, which became an organization known as the Green Belt Movement (GBM). GBM has now "assisted women in planting more than 40 million trees on community lands including farms, schools, and church compounds."[8]

With trees, education, and helping communities take ownership of the problems they're facing and discover solutions, Maathai's work is not just about developing the environment, but also leaders. In her Nobel Lecture, Maathai shared that her hope was that her work "will encourage [women] to raise their voices and take more space for leadership."[9]

Maathai took large, overwhelming problems—poverty and deterioration of the environment—and focused on one little thing she could do to help. "It's the little things citizens do. That's what will make the difference. My little thing is planting trees."[10] And although "her work was often considered both unwelcome and subversive in her own country, where her outspokenness constituted stepping far outside traditional gender roles,"[11] Maathai pressed forward. She knew that her work wasn't impacting a few farmers or a few schools, but generations who would be able to have even greater opportunities because one woman cared enough to do something small that would make a big difference.

Beulah Louise Henry

"I invent because I cannot help myself." Said without apology by Beulah Louise Henry (born in North Carolina in 1887), who was a self-taught engineer and inventor. She received 49 patents on her more than 100 inventions between 1912 and her death in 1973. Nicknamed "Lady Edison," Henry was inventing and creating at the age of nine, and her work resulted in new toys, cleaning products, household items, and even a typewriter attachment. Her ideas were thoughtful, practical, and gave her the opportunity not only to make a living from her inventions, but to open two businesses in New York City and work as a consultant for other businesses.[12]

At a time in history "when few people, especially women, were able to make money off their inventions," Henry made it her career. She proved that, even without formal training, women could succeed as engineers, and that people wanted—and would purchase—"practical inventions that solved everyday problems."[13]

Henry was a leader who knew what she wanted and how to make it happen. She surrounded herself with a team who could help bring her inventions to life, directed the production of her products, and confidently pursued her passions. What does it take for someone to use their creativity to invent? Henry claimed that all anyone needs to invent "is time, space and freedom."[14] She was making the world a better place, one creative, kind act at a time.

Imagine what we could do if we stopped apologizing unnecessarily and started using our words, creativity, inspiration, imagination, and talents to confidently do the work we've been created to do. What would we be known for, at the end of our lives, if we quieted the shoulds the world blasts at us and instead chose to pursue the work God has for us—whether anyone has done it before or not? Who might we inspire in the future as they look back on the work we do now, the words we use, the forgiveness we offer, or the faith we share? Let's stop apologizing for taking up the space God has given us, surround ourselves with people who can help us make our dreams a reality, and do whatever small, creative, empowering act we can to make a difference.

Junko Tabei

Our attempts to overcome worry and silence the shouts that tell us we should just be "happier" can feel like a long, slow climb up a very large mountain. It takes practice to do this well and a guide to help us accomplish our task the right way—not the quick and easy way.

Junko Tabei knew a thing or two about climbing mountains. The Japanese mountaineer was the first woman to summit Mount Everest as well as the highest mountain on each of the seven continents—the Seven Summits.

Born in 1939, Tabei's passion for mountain climbing started as a child. As a young adult she formed a women's climbing club, a group of women who, on their first expedition, forged a new path on a 24,786-foot mountain.[15] Tabei survived incredible obstacles—including being buried under an avalanche, running out of funding, and struggling to obtain the necessary permissions—on her quest to conquer the tallest mountains in the world. From Everest to Denali, Kilimanjaro to Puncak Jaya, Tabei pursued her passion, set records, and inspired countless women to climb whatever "mountain" they were facing.

After years of humble focus, hard work, and dedication, Tabei crossed the Seven Summits off her list—and then she went on to attempt to climb the highest mountain in every country, conquering 76 of them.

Tabei's two children grew up watching their mother pursue what she loved as she shared her passion and expertise with others. By quieting the shout of should that told her mountain climbing wasn't for women, Junko Tabei was able to leave a legacy that has allowed other women to embrace the wonder and thrill of reaching their own summits.

The mountains we face may not be as literal as Kilimanjaro, but we can use Tabei's example—and her words—as an encouragement to take that next step on our journey to swap worry for wonder: "Do not give up. Keep on your quest."[16]

Kathrine Switzer

In 1967, Kathrine Switzer finished the Boston Marathon. A feat of tremendous athletic and mental endurance, Switzer's accomplishment was a significant milestone for female athletes—she was the first woman ever to enter,* run, and finish the famous marathon. Previously, the Boston Marathon was considered too challenging for women. Switzer shares in her memoir, "The marathon was made a part of Patriots' Day in 1897, the year after the revival of the Olympic Games in Athens. Several young men…returned home [from Athens] fascinated with a romantic new event called the marathon." The Boston Marathon is special, she explains, because of its historical importance—and she "was going to be a part of history!"[17]

As Switzer's father once said, "Life is for participating, not spectating."[18] But Switzer would make history, documented in black-and-white photographs, when a race official attempted to pull her off the course. Journalists followed along, waiting for her to give up or prove that the run was a publicity stunt. Switzer finished the marathon and went on to run another thirty-plus marathons, including winning the women's division in the New York City marathon in 1974, just two years after women were officially allowed to enter it. Fifty years after her first historic race in Boston, Switzer again finished the Boston Marathon at age 70.

---

* Bobbi Gibb is recognized as the first woman to run the Boston Marathon (in 1966) and finished an hour ahead of Switzer's time. Unlike Switzer, however, Gibb was not officially entered in the race.

Switzer never set out to change the landscape of sports for women, but as she silenced the shouts that told her what women could and should do, she paved the way for generations of women who would be able to freely and openly pursue their passions and talents.

The work you do today may not seem significant compared to what others around you are accomplishing, but your faithfulness to run the race set before you (see Hebrews 12:1-3) might just be the example someone needs to say "yes" to God. The progress you make today may be the first step in God's larger plan to advance His kingdom in ways you will never see.

In fact, Switzer shares that "in 1967, few would have believed that marathon running would someday attract millions of women, become a glamour event in the Olympics and on the streets of major cities, help transform views of women's physical ability and help redefine their economic roles in traditional cultures."[19] She ran because she loved running—the longer, the better. Now her legacy has changed how the world views marathons and the women who run them.

Amelia Earhart

I have always been fascinated by Amelia Earhart. I remember reading about her travels and her mysterious disappearance in elementary school, and I was so in awe of this woman who would try things that had never been done before. It's no surprise to me that Earhart was the kind of child who ignored social expectations and did what she loved—climbing trees, fishing, playing hard, and hunting rats. But she was also growing up in a time when women were beginning to defy the odds and enter fields they had never accessed before. So Earhart saved newspaper clippings about successful women in male-dominated fields, including film directors and producers, lawyers, and women in advertising, management, and even engineering. Inspiration from women around the country would help one little girl believe that she could not only dream of flying but could also make that dream come true.

Six months after her first flying lesson in 1921, Earhart had saved enough money to buy her first plane. She would fly that plane to 14,000 feet—the first woman to fly so high. In 1928 she became the first woman to fly across the Atlantic. Just four years later, she repeated the feat, this time solo—only the second person to have done so. From ticker-tape parades to meeting the president, breaking records and being the first woman to receive the Distinguished Flying Cross from Congress, Earhart cleared the way for women around the world to swap doubt and discouragement for dreaming.

In 1937, Earhart set off to become the first woman to fly around the world. She had spent nearly a decade changing the idea of what was possible for a woman, and she had her sights set on this last incredible goal. Although every plan was in place, every precaution taken—down to United States ships lighting the way during a particularly challenging part of the journey—Earhart and her navigator, Fred Noonan, disappeared. A rescue attempt "became the most extensive air and sea search in naval history." Reluctantly, after spending $4 million and searching 250,000 square miles of ocean, the United States government ended the search.[20]

Earhart quieted the shouts of should that told her girls had to behave a certain way and only hold certain jobs. Earhart dreamed big—bigger than anything that had ever been done before—and didn't wait for anyone to set an example so she could compare her progress to theirs. We weren't all created to be trailblazers, but we can all open our hearts to the wild, audacious dreams God has for us. While we're still on this earth, God has work for us to do, and we can pursue it passionately.

You may never win awards for the goals and dreams you accomplish in the name of Jesus, but you could be the one person someone else looks up to as they take their own next steps of faith.

Mother Teresa

Did you know that Mother Teresa struggled with doubt? We share this Nobel Peace Prize winner's inspiring quotes online and know the highlights of her ministry serving the poor, but you might not know that she wrote the following:

> In my heart there is no faith—no love—no trust—
> there is so much pain—the pain of longing, the pain
> of not being wanted.—I want God with all the pow-
> ers of my soul—and yet there between us—there is terri-
> ble separation.—I don't pray any longer—I utter words
> of community prayers—and try my utmost to get out of
> every word the sweetness it has to give.—But my prayer
> of union is not there any longer.—I no longer pray.—
> My soul is not one with You—and yet when alone in the
> streets—I talk to You for hours—of my longing for You.[21]

But she never let her doubts or struggles with loneliness keep her from doing the work God had called her to do. The part of her story we know best—how she served the poor in India—was something she began when she was 38, after teaching at Saint Mary's High School in Calcutta for 17 years. With no finances to help her get started, Mother Teresa used her gifts of teaching to start a school for the children living in the slums. Two years later she started the Missionaries of Charity, an organization that today has branches in Europe, Asia, Africa, Latin America, North America, and Australia as they carry out Mother Teresa's mission to "love and care for those persons nobody was prepared to look after."[22]

When we quiet the shout of what we should feel or how we should act when it comes to our faith and instead choose to obey God, even through our doubts and fears, we can make a difference in His kingdom. We can doubt but trust God. We can fear but walk forward in faith. We can wonder if it's too late to start but remain alert for what God has next.

Chapter 1—I Should Be More Like Her

1. Debbie Hampton, "How Your Thoughts Change Your Brain, Cells, and Genes," *The Best Brain Possible*, December 13, 2015, http://thebestbrainpossible.com/how-your-thoughts-change -your-brain-cells-and-genes.

2. John MacArthur, *The MacArthur New Testament Commentary: Acts 13–28* (Chicago: Moody, 1996), 91-92.

3. Ibid., 92.

4. Matthew Henry, "Verses 6-15," *Matthew Henry's Commentary: Acts, Bible Gateway* (abridgment from the public domain), accessed January 21, 2020, http://www.biblegateway.com/resources /matthew-henry/Acts.16.6-Acts.16.15.

5. MacArthur, *MacArthur New Testament Commentary*, 95-96.

6. Henry, "Verses 6-15."

Chapter 2—I Should Be a Better Mother

1. Andrea Diaz, "Officials Release Video from Gender Reveal Party That Ignited a 47,000-Acre Wildfire," *CNN*, with contributions from Amir Vera, last updated November 28, 2018, http:// www.cnn.com/2018/11/27/us/arizona-gender-reveal-party-sawmill-wildfire-trnd/index.html.

2. Rebecca Webber, "The Comparison Trap," *Psychology Today*, November 7, 2017, last reviewed September 4, 2019, http://www.psychologytoday.com/us/articles/201711/the-comparison-trap.

3. Amanda Bible Williams, "Bowed in Worship," *She Reads Truth Bible* (Nashville, TN: Holman Bible, 2017), 405.

Chapter 3—I Should Have More Friends

1. Suzanne Degges-White, as quoted in Alia Hoyt and Molly Edmonds, "What Is Friendship?," *HowStuffWorks*, last updated August 29, 2018, http://people.howstuffworks.com/what-is-friend ship.htm.

2. "Proverbs 18:24," *Matthew Henry's Concise Commentary, Bible Hub*, accessed January 23, 2020, http://biblehub.com/commentaries/proverbs/18-24.htm.

3. Mark Strauss, ed., *Layman's New Testament Bible Commentary* (Uhrichsville, OH: Barbour, 2008), 230.

Chapter 4—I Should Have More Things by Now

1. Margo Aaron, "Why We Buy Things We Don't Need," *Medium,* October 9, 2016, http://medium .com/behavior-design/why-we-buy-things-we-dont-need-7d062fba98ab.

2. "The American Idea of Success," *Discover,* accessed January 24, 2020, http://www.discover.com /credit-cards/resources/the-american-idea-of-success.

3. Jeff Haden, "This Survey Shows People Need Four Things to Feel Successful (and They All Require a Lot of Money)," *Inc.*, January 26, 2018, http://www.inc.com/jeff-haden/this-survey-shows -people-need-4-things-to-feel-successful-and-they-all-require-a-lot-of-money.html.

Chapter 6—I Should Speak Up More/Less

1. Deborah Tannen, "The Truth About How Much Women Talk—and Whether Men Listen," *Time*, June 28, 2017, http://time.com/4837536/do-women-really-talk-more.

Chapter 7—I Should Apologize Less

1. Karina Schumann and Michael Ross, "Why Women Apologize More Than Men: Gender Differences in Thresholds for Perceiving Offensive Behavior," *Psychological Science* 21, no.11 (November 2010): 1649–1655, doi:10.1177/0956797610384150.

2. Nicolette Amarillas, "It's Time for Women to Stop Apologizing So Much," *Entrepreneur*, July 17, 2018, http://www.entrepreneur.com/article/314199.

3. Ibid.

4. Judith Tutin, "Do You Apologize Too Much? What You Need to Know About Saying Sorry," *YourTango*, February 21, 2018, accessed October 11, 2019, http://www.yourtango.com/experts /judith_tutin/do-you-apologize-too-much-4-ways-say-im-sorry.

Chapter 8—I Should Stop Worrying and Be Happier

1. Kylie Francis and Michel J. Dugas, "Assessing Positive Beliefs About Worry: Validation of a Structured Interview," *Personality and Individual Differences* 37, no. 2 (July 2004): 405–415, http://doi .org/10.1016/j.paid.2003.09.012.

2. "Sleep and Mental Health," *Harvard Mental Health Letter*, *Harvard Health Publishing*, July 2009, last updated March 18, 2019, http://www.health.harvard.edu/newsletter_article/sleep-and -mental-health.

Chapter 9—I Should Work Less and Serve More

1. Rafael Tonon, "How Mugaritz's Provocative Tasting Menu Comes Together," *Eater*, April 25, 2018, http://www.eater.com/2018/4/25/17219450/mugaritz-restaurant-spain-basque-country -menu-creative-process.

2. "Burn-Out an 'Occupational Phenomenon': International Classification of Diseases," *Mental Health*, *World Health Organization*, May 28, 2019, http://www.who.int/mental_health/evidence /burn-out/en.

3. Stephanie Watson, "Volunteering May Be Good for Body and Mind," *Harvard Health Blog*, *Harvard Health Publishing*, June 26, 2013, last updated October 29, 2015, http://www.health.harvard .edu/blog/volunteering-may-be-good-for-body-and-mind-201306266428.

4. Tremper Longman, ed., *Layman's Old Testament Bible Commentary* (Uhrichsville, OH: Barbour, 2010), 22.

5. "How Big Was Noah's Ark?," *Ark Encounter*, accessed January 30, 2020, http://arkencounter.com /noahs-ark/size.

6. Longman, *Layman's Old Testament*, 24.

Chapter 10—I Should Have Achieved That Dream by Now

1. Jesse Carey, "The Before You're 40 Bucketlist," *Relevant*, March 3, 2016, http://relevantmagazine .com/life5/youre-40-bucketlist.

2. Longman, *Layman's Old Testament*, 67.

3. Ibid., 72.

Chapter 11—I Should Pray More

1. Bruce Hurt, "Prayer—Greek Words for Prayer," *Precept Austin*, last updated August 28, 2016, http://www.preceptaustin.org/prayer-greek_words_for_prayer.

2. Charles L. Quarles, study notes on Matthew 6:9-11, in *HCSB Study Bible*, ed. Edwin A. Blum and Jeremy Royal Howard (Nashville, TN: Holman Bible, 2010), 1622-1623.

3. A.W. Tozer, *Prayer: Communing with God in Everything* (Chicago: Moody, 2016), 12.

Chapter 12—I Should Never Doubt What God Has Planned for Me

1. Charles Haddon Spurgeon, "The Desire of the Soul in Spiritual Darkness," *The New Park Street Pulpit*, vol. 1 (London: Passmore and Alabaster, 1856), 239.

2. Longman, *Layman's Old Testament*, 1335.

3. Raechel Myers, "Identity Crisis," *She Reads Truth Bible* (Nashville, TN: Holman Bible, 2017), 1440.

4. Longman, *Layman's Old Testament*, 1337.

5. Ibid.

Appendix—Women Who Silenced Should

1. Bryan R. Swopes, "26 October 1944," *This Day in Aviation: Important Dates in Aviation History*, October 26, 2019, http://www.thisdayinaviation.com/tag/tommy-tompkins.

2. Ibid.

3. "Ada Lovelace Biography," *Biography*, April 2, 2014, last updated July 18, 2019, http://www.bio graphy.com/scholar/ada-lovelace.

4. Ibid.

5. "Rehema House," *Mercy House Global*, accessed February 1, 2020, http://mercyhouseglobal.org /rehema-house.

6. "Mercy House Makers," *Mercy House Global*, accessed October 9, 2019, http://mercyhouseglobal .org/mercy-house-makers.

7. "Biography," *Wangari Maathai, The Green Belt Movement*, accessed October 11, 2019, http://www .greenbeltmovement.org/wangari-maathai/biography.

8. "Wangari Maathai," *Nobel Women's Initiative*, accessed October 11, 2019, http://nobelwomens initiative.org/laureate/wangari-maathai.

9. "Wangari Maathai—Nobel Lecture," *The Nobel Prize*, December 10, 2004, accessed February 1, 2020, http://www.nobelprize.org/prizes/peace/2004/maathai/26050-wangari-maathai-nobel -lecture-2004.

10. "Wangari Maathai," *Nobel Women's Initiative.*

11. "Wangari Maathai," *Encyclopædia Britannica*, September 21, 2019, accessed February 1, 2020, http://www.britannica.com/biography/Wangari-Maathai.

12. "Getting to Know…Beulah Louise Henry," *Tar Heel Tidbits, Carolina Country*, August 2013, accessed October 11, 2019, http://www.carolinacountry.com/carolina-stories/tar-heel-lessons /getting-to-know-beulah-louise-henry.

13. Roxanna Coldiron, "Meet Beulah Louise Henry: She Invented the Bobbinless Sewing Machine," *Martha Stewart*, March 6, 2018, http://www.marthastewart.com/1526370/beulah-louise -henry-invented-bobbinless-sewing-machine.

14. Beulah Louise Henry, as quoted in Autumn Stanley, *Mothers and Daughters of Invention: Notes for a Revised History of Technology* (New Brunswick, NJ: Rutgers University Press, 1995), 422.

15. Patricia Bauer, "Junko Tabei," *Encyclopædia Britannica*, November 28, 2016, last updated October 16, 2019, http://www.britannica.com/biography/Tabei-Junko.

16. Junko Tabei, as quoted in Brad Frenette, "A Final Interview with Junko Tabei," *Outside*, October 20, 2017, http://www.outsideonline.com/2252936/junko-tabei-anniversary.

17. Kathrine Switzer, *Marathon Woman: Running the Race to Revolutionize Women's Sports* (Boston, MA: Da Capo, 2017), 80-81.

18. Ibid., 9.

19. Kathrine Switzer, as quoted in Victor Mather, "First Woman to Enter Boston Marathon Runs It Again, 50 Years Later," *The New York Times*, April 17, 2017, http://www.nytimes.com/2017/04/17 /sports/boston-marathon-kathrine-switzer.html.

20. "Biography," *Amelia Earhart*, accessed November 14, 2019, http://www.ameliaearhart.com /biography.

21. Mother Teresa, in a letter sent to Father Picachy, September 3, 1959, in *Mother Teresa: Come Be My Light: The Private Writings of the "Saint of Calcutta"* (New York: Doubleday, 2007), 193.

22. "Mother Teresa—Biographical," *The Nobel Prize*, accessed November 12, 2019, http://www.nobel prize.org/prizes/peace/1979/teresa/biographical.

About the Author

Crystal Stine encourages women to pursue a life of less that leads to more. Along with being a popular speaker, she is the author of *Holy Hustle: Embracing a Work-Hard, Rest-Well Life*, has had her writing featured in dozens of national and international magazines and websites, and has appeared on countless podcasts. Crystal is also the author of *Creative Basics* and the creator of the "Clarity Coaching" course, and she served as managing editor of *Craving Connection* by the (in)courage team. Crystal lives in Pennsylvania with her husband and daughter.

Connect with Crystal at
www.crystalstine.me

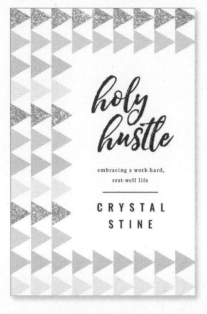

Holy Hustle
Work without Shame,
Rest without Guilt

Balance. It's what we long for in our lives as we hear shouts of "Work harder!" in one ear and whispers to "rest more" in the other. What if God's plan for us isn't just one way or the other?

Enter the *holy hustle*.

Crystal Stine followed the path to success as she climbed the corporate ladder. Now she explores "hustle" in a new light as a self-employed, work-from-home mom. She invites you to join her in experiencing...

- *renewed peace* as you focus on serving, not striving

- *reawakened potential* as you ditch comparison and embrace community

- *redefined purpose* as you seek the roles God has for you

You were created to work with enthusiasm for the right reasons—and you were also made with a need to rest. Discover the places where these two sides meet in a happy, holy hustle.